70 Life's Lessons

By Scott Paulson

Copyright 2019 Scott F. Paulson

All rights reserved. No portion of this book may be used or reproduced by any means, graphic, electronic or mechanical, including photocopying, recording, taping or by any information storage retrieval system, without the written permission of the publisher except in the case of brief quotations embodied in critical articles or reviews.

Dedication

To my parents, Fred and Ronelva, for without them, neither this book nor I would exist.

Table of Contents

Introduction

Chapter One: Be Persistent

Chapter Two: Walk

Chapter Three: Don't engage in jealousy

Chapter Four: Share

Chapter Five: Don't be mean

Chapter Six: Handle disappointment appropriately

Chapter Seven: Be patient

Chapter Eight: Pursue your dreams

Chapter Nine: Don't bully or allow others to bully you

Chapter Ten: Develop your gift

Chapter Eleven: Tell the truth

Chapter Twelve: Have hands-on experiences

Chapter Thirteen: Enjoy life's simple pleasures

Chapter Fourteen: Take time for God or another power every day

Chapter Fifteen: Set goals

Chapter Sixteen: Keep a calendar

Chapter Seventeen: Don't show that you're upset

Chapter Eighteen: Trust mom's advice

Chapter Nineteen: Document practically everything

Chapter Twenty: Speak well

Chapter Twenty-One: Realize the importance of family

Chapter Twenty-Two: Be yourself

Chapter Twenty-Three: Teach the children well

Chapter Twenty-Four: Diversify your jobs

Chapter Twenty-Five: Respect people

Chapter Twenty-Six: Keep it lighthearted

Chapter Twenty-Seven: Let people know what you want

Chapter Twenty-Eight: Reject racism

Chapter Twenty-Nine: Value true friendships

Chapter Thirty: Decide if love is for you

Chapter Thirty-One: Stay out of debt

Chapter Thirty-Two: Balance time for self, others, and work

Chapter Thirty-Three: Don't be overly satisfied

Chapter Thirty-Four: Read

Chapter Thirty-Five: Write

Chapter Thirty-Six: Listen

Chapter Thirty-Seven: Don't let frustrations ruin your day

Chapter Thirty-Eight: Don't brag

Chapter Thirty-Nine: Promote yourself properly

Chapter Forty: Practice moderation

Chapter Forty-One: Have proper timing in your life

Chapter Forty-Two: Don't waste money

Chapter Forty-Three: Discipline yourself

Chapter Forty-Four: Accept change when it can likely make improvements

Chapter Forty-Five: Use social media with care

Chapter Forty-Six: Smile

Chapter Forty-Seven: Don't hold a grudge

Chapter Forty-Eight: Ignore ignorance

Chapter Forty-Nine: Give people a second chance

Chapter Fifty: Continue learning

Chapter Fifty-One: Know yourself

Chapter Fifty-Two: Get a second opinion

Chapter Fifty-Three: See a doctor

Chapter Fifty-Four: Avoid things that harm you

Chapter Fifty-Five: Own your mistakes

Chapter Fifty-Six: Take risks when they likely can't harm you

Chapter Fifty-Seven: Be inclusive

Chapter Fifty-Eight: Get up and out every day

Chapter Fifty-Nine: Be informed and share knowledge, thoughts, and beliefs

Chapter Sixty: Compliment people

Chapter Sixty-One: Be happy

Chapter Sixty-Two: Be generous

Chapter Sixty-Three: Just do it

Chapter Sixty-Four: Realize you are dispensable

Chapter Sixty-Five: Write a last will and testament

Chapter Sixty-Six: Have experiences

Chapter Sixty-Seven: Be trustworthy

Chapter Sixty-Eight: Realize the past is gone

Chapter Sixty-Nine: Be grateful

Chapter Seventy: Learn to say no

Momisms

Conclusion

About the Author

Introduction

Five years ago, I wrote a book titled "65 Life's Lessons: The Most Important Lesson from Each Year of My Life (including Momisms)." At that time, I wrote that becoming a senior can be traumatic due to society's traditional labeling and expectations of one reaching the milestone in his or her life. As my senior status quickly approached, I chose to face it head-on with reflections on the best things I had learned about living during my first six-and-a-half decades. Now that I am nearly 70 years of age, I have updated the book and added five more lessons to the book. As with the first edition, I sincerely believe readers will find the lessons accompanied by my personal experiences to be beneficial as well as often enlightening. Many of the lessons that I have learned are right on the calendar mark throughout my life. Others are approximately timed. The intent is more than to simply share life's learned lessons, but also to tell about the experiences that have taught me the lessons. In other words, this is not a philosophy of life. It is much more personal. This writing is a memoir accompanied by the best of what life has taught me so far.

Be forewarned that these are not the sugar-coated life's lessons or philosophies of life that people have often heard or read. These lessons are from real living which isn't always sweet. While the Golden Rule, do unto others as you would have them do unto you, applies most of the time, there are times people need to treat others on their own terms. There are times people may get walked on if they don't tweak the age-old philosophies of life via some realistic lessons for living a good life.

Enjoying and engaging in the craft of writing is something I have done since I was a youngster. Being very analytical in many things I do, it is only natural that I have come to write this book. When I have had successes, as hopefully we have all had, it is in me to share my successes so that others may have similar successes. When wounded, as all of us have likely been, it is in me to become a warrior for others. I have learned from my struggles and know that sharing what I have learned from my mistakes and misfortunes is possible by writing about them. In the following pages, I'm sharing some things about life that I wish were shared with me during my life's journey.

The lessons shared in these pages were learned from the year I was born through the present. Never having been much of a procrastinator when it comes to my writing, I began the first edition of this book, "65 Life's Lessons," one month before I became a senior citizen. I began this edition, "70 Life's Lessons," four months before turning 70 years old. The goal at the outset of writing "65 Life's Lessons," which I achieved, was to complete the book during my sixty-fifth year of life. The editing was completed sometime after that time. My more stringent goal in writing "70 Life's Lessons," which I also achieved, was to complete the update and expansion of the book by my 70th birthday. In this second edition, as was intended in the first edition, I sincerely believe readers will find usefulness and, often times, enlightening passages in the book. Entries include memorable references as to how I learned the life's lessons, whether I learned a lesson on my own, by observing others, or by interacting with others.

If you know me and think you recognize yourself somewhere in the book, you may be right. Then again, maybe it's someone else. I know and have known many people. Names of persons referred to in the essays, in most instances, are withheld as it is not my intent to embarrass or praise anyone, other than myself at times. Additionally, I would never reveal any confidences people may have shared with me throughout my life. Of course, such written statements in the introduction of the book should ward off any lawsuits as well. Like I said, I'm analytical in most everything I do.

You are my target audience. My target audience includes all ages, which includes younger people who are currently creating their lifetime goals and striving to achieve them. They can learn from my subjunctive voice regarding life. My target audience also includes older people who will likely read the book with interest to see how my life's lessons compares to their own.

Beyond updating and editing the text of the former book about my life's lessons, and beyond adding five more life's lessons, I have added additional Momisms, which are sometimes called Mom's Wisdom. Lastly, I have trimmed the lengthy title of the first book from 13 words to three words, "70 Life's Lessons." I believe the more reasonable length of the title is just one of a good number of improvements over the previous edition.

Chapter One

Be persistent

In the first year of my life, I am quite certain that I would have learned to be persistent. It's a lesson that newborns learn, regardless of how unknowingly it is learned at the time. Though I would have been unaware of the life's lesson at the time, it is one that has been everlasting. Being persistent is a lesson that has had, and will continue to have, relevance and importance throughout my entire life, just as all of the early lessons in life have had lasting relevance.

Though it was obviously a long time ago, I learned that being persistent can be beneficial to me. As a newborn, that persistence is achieved by engaging in continued fussing until wants and needs are met. In time, fortunately, the method of acquiring needs changes drastically just as the needs change greatly. Though the methods involved in obtaining wants and needs change throughout one's lifetime, persistence is a constant, valuable tool.

Chapter Two

Walk

From what I have been told, by the age of one I had been engulfed in the fascinating process of learning to walk. Though often taken for granted, learning to walk is one of the most impactful skills a person can ever acquire. Undeniably, walking is one of the first things in life that a person strives to achieve. As a senior citizen, walking becomes one of the most important activities a person strives to maintain. Every one of my steps, from my first steps to the steps that will be taken throughout my senior years, is the ultimate travelogue of my life. Merely thinking about where walking has taken me as I have journeyed through my life thus far is an incredible thought.

Walking to maintain mobility is something I have disciplined myself to do most every day as it is a skill I have learned not to take for granted. In 2007, a back problem followed by an operation on a herniated disk disrupted my ability to walk easily and comfortably for a time. That medical experience taught me never to take the ability to walk for granted. Admittedly, I had not thought much about the importance of walking until I had the back problem accompanied by the challenges I faced in walking.

The last day I taught school before totally retiring from teaching in May of 2013, I took my final long walk from my classroom to the office and then to my car to go home. As I was walking, I reasoned that I wouldn't be walking as much as I had been walking while I was working unless I set a goal for myself. That's when I promised myself I would walk most every day to keep myself mobile. Since that last day of teaching, whether it's raining out or the sun is shining, whether there is 90-degree blistering heat or 10-degree frigid temperatures, whether it is Christmas or another important day in my life, I vehemently make an effort to walk. On very rare occasions, I have had to skip a day for one reason or another. The few times I have missed a day, I have made a conscious effort to take two walks on the following day, one early in the day and another later in the day. I have averaged at least one walk a day since I retired from teaching. Currently, my walks are a minimum of 20 minutes. Incidentally, I am not a huge fan of total retirement. Therefore, I continue to keep physically active by doing part-time jobs, which has often included doing delivery work. Additionally, as this book and many other books I have written attests, my penchant for writing keeps me very busy after having retired from teaching as well. Walking, occasionally working part-time, and writing are my methods of avoiding boredom in retirement, or should I more accurately say, semi-retirement.

Of the walking, I tired quickly of the treadmill. Consequently, I walk outside when the weather is agreeable. In fact, I prefer walking outdoors so much more than indoors that I often walk outdoors when the weather isn't very agreeable. It is when I walk outdoors that I most often remember to take deep breaths as deep breathing has many benefits. Deep breathing, so I have read, reduces stress by relaxing one's mind and body while increasing one's energy level. Another bonus to breathing deep is that it is a natural painkiller. It also improves one's blood flow, which naturally is a positive. By bringing large amounts of oxygen into one's body during exercise, carbon dioxide is detoxified from within. Of the many other benefits, it reduces inflammation and improves the digestive system.

When the weather is totally uncooperative with the walking demands I have placed on myself, however, I drive to a mall or a large department store and walk without stopping to get my exercise. When all else fails, however, I have treadmills available to me at my residence and a nearby health club of which I have a free membership through my health insurance plan, which is a nice senior's advantage. Anyway, I highly recommend such a routine for maintaining or improving one's health. Beyond the physical benefits, a good walk can clear one's mind. Walking does a body and a mind a great deal of good.

Chapter Three

Don't engage in jealousy

Some people think of a two-year-old child as being in what is developmentally termed 'the terrible twos.' By definition, 'the terrible twos' is characterized as a child alternating between reliance on his or her parents and experimenting with a desire to be independent. This is said to be normal in a child's development. I assume that I lived up to that infamous reputation at that age. Compound 'the terrible twos' with being the youngest child in the family, which is often equated to the baby of the family being spoiled. I had a sister who was 23 months older. There were no other siblings in the family when I was two years old, and there would not be another sibling until I was five-and-a-half years old. Therefore, I can assume that when I was two, I would have subconsciously learned how to deal with a jealous person who was seeing me get the bulk of the attention in the family. Of course, I was too young to know that I was probably monopolizing my parents' attention. Yet, the older sibling would have possibly been jealous or resentful of my getting the attention.

Naturally, as time passed, there were times I was the jealous child. Due to my sister being older, I eventually became jealous of her because there were things she could do at her age that I wasn't allowed do at my age, such as going to school and taking swimming lessons. A great frustration was when she joined the school band and began playing the clarinet. I wasn't allowed to join when she did because I was too young to satisfy the age requirement dictated by the school's band director.

Some five years after I was born, my brother was born. Naturally, I had to take seconds to the new guy in the family. I might add that my sister was always a very sweet girl, which made her very popular with everyone, including me. Sweet, incidentally, is an adjective that never described my brother or me. Therefore, beyond having a spoiled younger brother to be jealous of for a time, I had my sister, who I saw as eternally being daddy's girl, owning the envied and coveted position of the most spoiled child. To be honest, all three of us were loved and spoiled a lot. However, if there was a least spoiled child, I am fairly certain that I was the one. Anyway, those initial experiences in life that involve jealousy should be expected and are a big part of the formative years. While jealousy is part of being very young, it is also part of the mixed emotions through life.

After having matured, if someone acts jealous of me, I try to feel glad that they think I have something of which to be jealous, and I move on without dwelling on the other person's jealousy. Contrarily, if I feel a tendency to be jealous of someone else, I either figure out what I can do to obtain what they have that I want, or I accept that obtaining what the other person has isn't possible for me. Then, I move on. Jealousy, I have come to realize, is a waste of time. Yet, admiring others can be a positive trait, and I do admire many people for their accomplishments. Being jealous of what others have, however, is not productive. It is good not to compare yourself to others. Instead, be content with what you have in life while working at achieving more of what you want. At any time in life, avoiding jealousy will make one's life better.

Chapter Four

Share

Share just as I am sharing my life's lessons with people who choose to read them. As far as this lesson being remembered as a three-year-old, to be honest, I don't think anyone remembers much of anything about being three years old. Some people claim to have vivid memories from an incredibly early age. Though debatable, I believe people who insist they remember events that happened when they were so very young may have heard about certain instances so many times that they start believing that they actually remember it having happened. Incredibly, some people claim to remember something they did sixty-some years ago when they were a three-year-old but then couldn't remember to show up for a meeting at two o'clock yesterday afternoon.

When I was three, I can only imagine that talk from my parents about sharing with others would have started to have had an impact on my behavior. By three, I was no doubt being taken out in public and allowed to roam a bit, which would have involved interacting with other people besides my parents and my sister. In interacting with other children, the need to share space, toys, food, another person's attention, and most everything else becomes one of the biggest challenges for a youngster. Naturally, learning to share is something that can be tough to do, or even want to do, throughout life. Yet, it needs to be done in order to survive life beyond the life of a hermit.

No doubt, the United States' form of government demands that those who have a great deal must share with those who do not have a great deal via the tax systems and governmental programs. The Bible makes a pitch for sharing with the have-nots as well. So, at a very young age, hopefully the lesson about sharing has begun because the need to share likely remains throughout life. Later in life, sharing goes beyond the sharing of material things and wealth. One should share their time, ideas, and knowledge, too. Imagine how far along society would not be if people didn't continually share, among other things, their ideas and knowledge.

Chapter Five

Don't be mean

It's never too early for a person to learn that he or she shouldn't be mean to people. I seemed to have taken joy in teasing my sister and, basically, being mean at times. Being a child, I didn't understand why I enjoyed doing it. In later years, it was pointed out to me by my mother that when I thought I was being funny, I was actually being an annoyance to others. So, I was sometimes told to stop the great amount of teasing I was doing as well as told to stop being mean. If I didn't stop, I would find out what being mean really was by being on the receiving end.

Of course, there is the vindictive type of being mean that exists, too. It's also never too early in life to learn that a person shouldn't be mean to people regardless of how much he may not like someone. I learned this at a young age via an incident that I can't erase from memory.

Through overhearing my mom's conversations with my dad about the neighbor lady who lived upstairs from us, I thought that the lady wasn't very nice. Back in the old days, it wasn't accepted for a man and woman to live together while not being married. My mom was suspicious that the couple, who were renting from my parents, wasn't married. This was revealed one day when a package came to our house. That evening after my dad got home from work, I overheard my mom telling my dad that the name on the package that had arrived for the neighbor lady had the lady's first name on it as well as a last name that was different from her husband's last name. Back in the day, a woman would almost always take her husband's last name when getting married. In another one of those conversations between my parents, my mom mentioned that the lady had a miscarriage and her baby wasn't going to be born after all.

After all I had overheard about the neighbor lady through my mom's conversations with my dad, I developed a dislike for the lady because my mom was so disapproving of her. One morning, the lady was in our kitchen having coffee with my mom, as she often did. I sat at the table and, as I often did, quietly listened. Then, out of the blue, most likely trying to make the lady feel bad since I didn't like her, I said, "Your baby died, didn't it?"

Wow, did I learn how to not be mean to people on that unforgettable day in my life! My mom perceived my comment as being mean. She must have also been undoubtedly embarrassed that the lady would have figured out that my mom had spoken about her to others in her absence and in front of me. Part of the punishment for my mean act involved a long day spent alone in my bedroom.

To finish the story, my mom must have finally found out for sure that the lady wasn't married to the man she lived with in the upstairs apartment as she told the couple that they had to live somewhere else. Yes, my mom was quite religious and wouldn't allow that sort of thing going on under her roof. Again, this occurred in the 1950s when one could, and often did, respond as my mother did. My interaction with the lady upstairs was my earliest recollection of being very mean to someone and learning that such behavior is not acceptable.

A side lesson involving this story is also that parents should watch what they say around children. As a child, I was living proof that a child listens. Worse than that, I was living proof that a child repeats what is heard.

Chapter Six

Handle disappointment appropriately

Handling disappointment is a very hard lesson to learn, especially at a young age when things are going pretty well in life for a child. Of course, if things aren't going well in one's life at a young age, a child probably doesn't even realize it as he doesn't know what other options are available to people yet. Nonetheless, I remember one of my first disappointments coming crashing down when I was just five years old. Having an older sister, I looked so forward to doing many things she got to do two years before I was allowed to do them because she was born almost two years before I was born. One of the things that she got to do that I couldn't wait to do was to attend kindergarten. Spending a few hours out of the house without Mom in control was definitely something I looked forward to having. Unfortunately, as local school finances would have it, the year I would have gone to kindergarten was the year it was canceled. Due to public discontent over the issue, as I recall, it was only cancelled for one year. Again, as bad luck would have it, the one year that kindergarten was not in session at the local school was the year I was five years old and would have gone. Therefore, my school life began the following year when I was at the proper age to be a first grader. I remember that my mother was disappointed by the cancellation of kindergarten that year, also. It very well could have been that she was looking forward to time without the control of a five-year-old just as much as I was looking forward to time without mom-control.

The assumed right to start school seemed to have been unjustly stripped from me. Yet, there was absolutely nothing I could do about it. Obviously, bitter disappointment is something that one faces over and over again throughout life. I learned that there are a number of ways of reacting to utter disappointment. One option is to be crabby about it day-in and day-out. Another option is to suffer in silence.

I'm quite sure I just suffered in silence over the disappointment because crabbing about it couldn't have changed anything in this situation. More than that, my mom didn't put up with my crabbiness as I would be summoned to my bedroom for the duration of my crabbiness.

I like to think that simply keeping disappointments to myself is still my way of handling most disappointments that can't be avoided. Many times when I complained, as I grew up, my mother would straightforwardly tell me, "Nobody wants to hear it!" Through the years, I have found that she was quite correct. Most often, nobody really wants to hear another person's complaints when there is absolutely nothing the listener can do to change the situation. I know I don't necessarily care to hear complaints of unpreventable situations that comes from others.

Of my kindergarten class being cancelled, in retrospect, I realize that my mother dealt with the unexpected disappointment extremely well. She made the best of it in a way that would help me and likely satisfy herself. While at home during that school year, I remember spending a lot of time at the kitchen table with my mom as she taught me to read, write, and do other academic activities. Educationally, she did not let the year go to waste. I remember her creating games I played and tests I took. I felt like I was in school that year after all, thanks to my mother's way of handling the disappointing circumstances. As with many of my life's most worthwhile lessons, my mother taught me this one by example.

Chapter Seven

Be patient

I learned how to sit still, or in more general terms, learned to be patient when I finally started going to school. More accurately, besides learning to be still, I most likely was forced to be more patient when adjusting to my new life as a school boy. Before going to school, my parents would likely have thought sitting still was not going to be very easy for me. Being patient, undoubtedly one of the most difficult lessons one must learn in life at an early age, can also be a hard lesson to put into practice later in life. While physical activities, such as sitting, come easier with age, being patient can be extremely difficult for some people throughout life. To this day, as difficult as it often is for me to be patient, I cautiously pride myself in having improved greatly in handling the life-long challenge. Living in a heavily-populated area my entire life, patience is nearly a near requirement when driving a car.

Be patient. Work at it. More than patience simply being an admirable trait that makes life easier for everyone, there are times it is required to co-exist with others.

Additionally, while doing many things in life, it is best to take time and enjoy the journey that is essential in achieving goals successfully. Naturally, besides goals not always being achieved easily, goals often don't happen quickly. With patience and effort, there are usually ways for a person to get reasonable things accomplished that he or she really wants to do. To reach goals in life, one likely has to build the road to get there. If one doesn't patiently develop the necessary groundwork to build a road that leads to successes and reached goals, life's goals will likely not be grasped. It's essential for a person to practice patience by taking the necessary time and by investing the needed effort that is required to reach the goals in life that truly matter to him or her.

Chapter Eight

Pursue your dreams

For a person to pursue his or her dreams and desires, it must be done with the persistence unknowingly practiced as an infant. It was in second grade that I insisted that I join the band as a trumpet player. After all, my sister was in the band and I knew I had it in me to make music just like she or any of those other band kids could do. The burning desire to be in the elementary school band was the first memory I have of a personal desire that refused to go away. It made no sense to me that a kid had to be in third grade and eight years old to play a musical instrument. I not only wanted to do it, but I knew that I could if I was given the chance. I pestered my parents about my need to join the band more than I had pestered them for anything before that time.

Finally, my mother convinced the band director to bend the rules and let me, a second grader, in the band. Even though the quite elderly band director had only allowed children, who were in the third grade or higher, join the band for as long as he had been running the music program, he let me in the band. I was so excited to be in the band that I didn't even mind too much that I got an antique steel clarinet instead of a shiny trumpet. I ended up with a clarinet because all the trumpets were taken. All the good clarinets made of wood were taken, too. Furthermore, I didn't even mind that I was the only boy in the huge clarinet section either. I just wanted to be in the band and to make music. It happened.

As it turned out, music became an enormous part of my life, and it all started with that desire to be in the band at a very early age. By sixth grade, I was second chair in the band's clarinet section, and by seventh grade, I was first chair. I remained there until I graduated from eighth grade. In high school, I was first chair. Then I was accepted to be in the School Band of America, which toured Europe when I was 18 years old. That achievement was followed with a music scholarship in college. In time, I would have many songs published, of which about a dozen were recorded by different recording artists. By pursuing a dream at the age of 7, much good came of the goal achieved by sheer persistence. When you want something so very much that is absolutely achievable, go for it!

Of course, sometimes persistence will turn around and hit you where it hurts. Going back to the time before I started school, probably three or four years of age, I was introduced to the bicycle with training wheels. Even at that age, I thought I was too big and was definitely too proud to be seen with training wheels on my bicycle. Therefore, I went outside on the sidewalk near the family house, somehow took the training wheels off, and started riding the two-wheeler like my older sister and the big kids in the neighborhood. In no time, I fell off the bike. Outside the back door of our house, there was a piece of metal attached to the sidewalk for scraping one's shoes off before entering the house. I scarcely noticed that piece of metal until I fell off my bike and split my head open on it. The bike ride ended as I swallowed my pride and went in the house to show my mother what I had done to my head without the training wheels on the bicycle. After a trip to the hospital for stitches, all was well. As for bicycle helmets, they were unheard of back in the 1950s, just as it was unheard of for me to do anything I perceived as childish when I was a youngster. Thinking back, I don't know why I was in such a hurry to grow up instead of just taking time to enjoy being the child I was. The lesson is to pursue dreams while being cautious and logical in the persistent pursuit.

## Chapter Nine

## Don't bully or allow others to bully you

Bullying is bad. It should neither be done by anyone nor tolerated by anyone. Bullies' goals are apparently to feel superior over their victims. Bullies attempt to make their victims miserable when they have no right to do so. When bullies victimize others, they should be stopped. The experts assert that bullies are lonely, insecure people who have bigger internal problems than they could likely give to those they prey upon. That, however, is not to say that they should be pitied at all. Join society's efforts to wipe out bullying. One way you can do so is by not permitting anyone to bully you. Bullies will find another victim when they realize that you will not allow them to bully you.

While a child has few choices as to his or her surroundings, an adult has control of his or hers. There is hardly any good reason for adults to allow anyone to bully them because they can often alter their surroundings and the people that are in their surroundings. When bullied, an adult can walk away or, possibly even better and more effectively, confront the abusive person. Either method tells the bully that his or her intended victim is not a person who will deliver his or her desired response to the bullying.

When a bully threatens, I've used the line, "Am I supposed to be scared or impressed?" After an eventful pause, I look them sternly in the eye and very assertively declare, "I am neither!" If it's in you to deliver these lines, feel free to borrow them.

The point is that the last thing you want to do with a bully is stand there and take the disrespectful treatment because your submission will be viewed by the bully as your weakness and his or her success. Whether you walk off, give a crushing response, get sarcastic, or even try to humor the bully by taking the high road, make sure your actions are unpredictable to the bully. If the person doesn't know how you'll react to his or her bulling in the future, you're not the passive target the bully needs for his or her dastardly acts. Do not show a bully that you are negatively impacted by his or her actions because that is exactly how the person wants and expects you to react. If you react negatively and show that you are upset, the bully will come back for more negative reactions from you. Upsetting you and receiving a negative reaction is what fuels a bully to continue bullying.

Dealing with bullies is not a quick and easy lesson for many people. For some, it takes a great amount of living to figure it out. That's why assisting children in dealing with horrendous bullying situations is sometimes appropriate, regardless of how much some claim that children should stand up for themselves. Don't go overboard in assisting a bullied child by taking total control of the situation, but use the occasion to teach the child how to handle a bully. Guide the child toward having success in dealing with the bullies he or she encounters. During such episodes in a child's upbringing, it is a good time to enforce the notion that, ideally, people are treated the way they allow others to treat them. The lesson is that no one has the right to treat anyone else badly or disrespectfully. When a person bullies, he or she deserves to be confronted, when it is safe for the bully's target to do so. Aptly, a bully should be left standing alone as his or her target exits the bully's failed exchange.

My earliest memories of being bullied occurred in elementary school. The first bullying incident occurred around third grade. I told no one I was being bullied, and I sincerely doubt that anyone noticed that I was being subjected to it. Likely feeling embarrassed that it was happening and not wanting to admit it to anyone, I suffered alone. There was this guy who didn't seem to care for me in my class. Why he didn't like me is still a mystery to me. I don't recall ever doing anything that deserved his dislike for me. Thinking back, what was not to like about me? I digress. An example of his bullying was when he let everyone but me cut in front of him for a drink of water at the hallway's water fountain during the class's bathroom break. I just stood and waited while everyone proceeded in front of him. Just before he took his drink of water after all the kids he let cut in line, he gave me an evil look, and then he enjoyed a long drink of his own. Then he gave me another evil look and slowly walked away. I was thinking 'why me, Lord,' several years before Kris Kristofferson wrote the song. When opportunities arose for him, he bullied me in other childish ways. In this earliest instance of being bullied, I used the ignore method by trying not to show that his actions really, really bothered me. In time, he quit doing this to me and actually became civil in time.

Fast-forward twenty years or so. This guy ended up running for political office. When we crossed paths at a local Fourth of July community event, he approached me with a big smile, shook my hand, gave me his political pitch and requested my vote. Without batting an eye, I mustered up an evil look, probably much like the one he used to give me back in the day, and moved on. Basically, I replaced my ignore method of his bullying with getting even and, whether right or wrong, I found awkward gratification in doing so.

I repeated the story about what a bully he was back in the day on numerous occasions before the election. More or less, I was helping his opponent, whoever he or she was, by default. The elementary school bully got trounced in that election as well as in following contests. Admittedly, I took great joy in seeing him get beat by embarrassing numbers. As experts say, many childhood bullies turn into unlikeable adults. As bad as this former bullying schoolmate got beat in the election, it is apparent that he turned into one of those unlikeable adults. By a great percentage, voters in the community obviously didn't care for him.

While there is obviously much to be said against holding a grudge, when dealing with a bully, not holding a grudge can possibly be tossed. A good rule of thumb regarding holding a grudge might be that if you've held a grudge against someone so long that you've forgotten what you were mad about, it's past time to forgive because you've obviously forgotten. Concerning other grudges that you remember forever and that eat at you for a long time, the notion of not holding the grudge can be debatable. Honestly, I consider forgiving in every instance, but sometimes a past pain makes it incredibly difficult.

Anyway, this childhood bully apparently had many other not-so-admirable characteristics as well. In the town where we lived, there was a no-tell motel right in its center. While it could be difficult not to pass the hotel if driving through town, the childhood bully-turned-failed politician had gained a reputation for hanging around the sleazy business. No big deal if you were single, I guess, but he was married at the time. Needless to say, I haven't kept up with the man through the years. The point is that he was a childhood bully who created bad habits that were apparently hard for him to break in adulthood. Yet, people should give a bully space to change his or her evil ways. The person either will change for the better or continue destroying himself or herself. Obviously, the choice is his or hers.

In another circumstance, when I was maybe eight years older and in high school, I had a summer job that was apparently lined up by my father. People I worked with obviously resented that I had a job that was setup for me. I worked at a typewriter shop and had a no-brainer job of cleaning typewriters. It involved using a small air gun to blow the crud out of the inside casing of the typewriter and then spraying a little oil to lubricate the keys' bars inside the casing. The two older men who worked in the back of the typewriter shop, especially the oldest and extremely obese guy, were incredibly mean to me. From what I gathered, they had been doing this job for a long, long time. While this was my summer job which would last some two-and-a-half months, they appeared to be doomed to this pathetic job for life. The older guy, tipping the scales at 350 pounds or more, must have resented that I got the job as an apparent favor to my father, as maybe he had known someone he would have rather had gotten the job. I don't know exactly what the man's problem was, but he definitely had a bitterness toward me. He would loudly insult me often when talking to the other full-time employee back in the work room. He never had the guts say throw his insults directly to me or when of his superiors at the business were present, but he would make sure I heard them. It was a situation in which an old man was continually and blatantly bullying me. One day, someone entered the shop and said to me, "I heard you on WLS Radio Saturday night! You sounded great"' I had been trying to be chosen as Art Roberts' Guest Teen DJ on WLS-AM radio that summer and had eventually been chosen. Shyly, I said to the person who complimented me, "Thanks. Glad you heard it." After that person left, the old man loudly said to the other full-time worker, "Pfft! Guest teen DJ on Chicago radio? The kid acts like he doesn't even know his name half the time." It was an entire summer of insults and bullying like this, and I suffered in silence as to not embarrass my dad by making a scene at his acquaintance's shop. Years later, I heard the old man had died, and I thought of what I once heard a lady say on Roe Conn's Chicago radio program one afternoon. When the lady spoke to the radio host about her ex-husband who had passed away, she said: "There comes a time when some people need to die."

Though somewhat vulgar, an example of being bullied as an adult is an incident that occurred when I was driving through the West Side of Chicago during one of my part-time summer jobs as a delivery person during my teaching years. At a corner on Chicago's West Side, I came to a complete stop at a stop sign. There was a young man, probably about 20-some years of age, who was apparently only there to intimidate people who happened by. As I looked in his direction, he degrading yelled, "What the fuck you lookin' at?" I surprised myself by looking right at him and yelling disgustedly with full voice, "A piece of shit! What's it to you?" By the stunned look on his face, it was obvious that he was shocked that I had actually stood up to his bullying. Since stifling him felt good, and I could see I had won the situation over, for good measure I repeated, "That's right, a piece of shit! That's what I'm lookin' at!"

As the incident at the West Side of Chicago street corner exemplifies, I started confronting bullies as an adult after having always ignored them when I was younger. Though I don't fight them tooth and claw, and I don't recommend that others do either, confronting them is the thing for me to do. In most instances, they show their underlying weakness by backing down immediately. In a recent case, I was surprised to encounter disrespect by a man I had helped out on a number of occasions in Chicago. I helped him out by giving him change or even dollars when he was panhandling on the street. One day I had absolutely no change on me and nothing smaller than a 20-dollar bill when he stopped me for money again. I explained, "Lo siento. No tengo cambio ahorita," which is Spanish for saying that I was sorry that I had no change at the moment. He turned to the guys he was standing with and started loudly insulting me as he and the others laughed. Not knowing his name, I loudly referred to him as "el mendigo," which is Spanish for the beggar. I proceeded to tell him in Spanish how I didn't appreciate his disrespect after all the times I had helped him in the past and that I would remember this incident of disrespect the next time he might ask me for money. The bullying beggar immediately stopped insulting me and stopped laughing at me. As he lowered his head and turned away from me, appearing to be embarrassed, his acquaintances stopped laughing as well. While doing part-time delivery jobs during my semi-retirement years, I have seen him several more times. The one time he called out to me and began to approach my vehicle, I nodded and drove on. I have decided that other needy persons in my travels can get my assistance instead. Again, either ignore or confront a bully.

Chapter Ten

Develop your gift

Positively, everyone is good at something. Beyond being good at something, if you have a gift, develop it. As a youngster, I realized that I stood out from others as a musician. It was apparent that many people were impressed at how I could pick up my clarinet and play all kinds of music. Beyond quickly having learned to read, play and even write music, I would hear a song on the radio or television and be able to play it quite readily. At first, I thought everyone who played a musical instrument could do it. In time, however, I learned by the reaction of my band director and parents that it was a gift few people have. My mom said that as a clarinetist, I was like my grandmother was at a piano. I was told that my grandmother could sit down at a piano and play any song she'd heard. Unlike me, my grandmother never learned how to read music.

Being just a kid, I didn't like working at the music or anything else all of the time. Instead of actually practicing the instrument by reading the music from books and sheet music, I would go in the family's basement and just play songs I liked without reading any music in front of me. Other times, I just created my own melodies. Even though I didn't often practice the music I was assigned to play in the school band or would be performing in music contests that I had been entered in by my parents or band director, I figured that I was improving my musical abilities just by playing the clarinet as often as I had.

My gift of music was my claim to fame not only as a youngster but in years to come, as I previously mentioned in another chapter about pursuing one's dreams. Other than spending time writing songs as a hobby with hopes of becoming successful at it someday, nurturing the gift of music ended at the end of my college years as I ended up majoring in English and education instead of music. I began an extremely demanding teaching career, accompanied by working financially-needed second jobs, which gave me very little time to do much more than work. Recognizing the gift and taking advantage of it as long as I had, though, is something I'm grateful for having done.

Deciding not to major in music in college and to not make it my lifelong career were decisions I made after my mother stated her strong opinions on my future. When I was in my third year of college, she sternly asked, "What are you going to do with a music degree in these times? Schools don't have much money and one of the first things they cut from their budgets is extra programs like music. You probably won't even be able to find a band director's job at a school. You need to work when you get out of school." I took her advice, and I believe time proved her right. I did not major in music or pursue any other type of music career other than maintaining aspirations to write popular songs someday. It is true that I unfortunately do not know how far I could have gone with a music career. Yet, by having taken my mother's advice, for decades I knew the job security of having a teaching position in a subject area in which there has always been a need. That job security and financial security have been comforting to me throughout my life. In spite of any missed opportunities in music, I have to believe that Mom was right. While teaching English has given me a good, lifelong career and purpose, my gift of music has given me great benefits throughout life including a great appreciation of and enjoyment from music. Again, embrace the gift you've been given and use it to some extent in your life.

Chapter Eleven

Tell the truth

I really, really try to tell the truth no matter how tempted I am to exaggerate a story or tell a lie about something. No matter how fantastic an exaggerated story could be, I avoid the accompanying guilt that comes with lying. Doing my best to stick to the facts when I tell a story has served me well.

Something happened to me when I was ten years old that I remember as the first time I was really tempted to tell a blatant lie. I always wanted to exaggerate the incident because it would have been so very extremely cool if the story had turned out differently. Yet, I never lied about it. The incident was one of those occurrences in life that I have never forgotten, and I never ever will forget it.

When John F. Kennedy was campaigning for the presidency of the United States, he visited my hometown. I always wanted to say that he spoke to me and shook my hand. The truth is that it almost happened. However, the bitter truth is that it didn't happen. As Kennedy's motorcade travelled through a strip mall where many people were anxiously waiting to see him, I was right on the edge of the sidewalk closest to the passing vehicles in the presidential hopeful's motorcade. When Kennedy's car crept by, I reached as far as I could with my hand actually over the car's siding. I was so close to him that I thought I was going to even touch him by shaking his hand. As he passed, both of his hands were occupied on the left side of the car and I was on the right. He turned and looked right at me with his brilliant eyes and incredible smile, but he never spoke to me or brought his hand over to my side of the car to shake my hand. I don't think he could have brought his hand to my side of the car at that moment even if he wanted to because people on the other side of the car had a hold of his hands.

I wanted so much for the story to be that he broke one hand away from the left side of his car so he could shake my hand. I wanted to be able to say that he did more than smile at me. It would have been a perfect part of the story to say that he actually said something to me as he smiled at me. These believable scenarios ran through my mind, but I could never bring myself to lie about it. I remember telling a school friend about the incident, and he excitedly asked, "Did he say anything to you?" I paused and admitted, "No, he just smiled at me." Oh, the temptation to lie about what almost happened. Through the years, I'm glad I didn't exaggerate the truth. I've lived with the truth that he looked at me, smiled, and if anything, communicated kindness with his eyes. Through this memory of being so tempted to lie, I learned that it feels good not submitting to temptation and not telling a lie. Instead, it's best to not exaggerate and to tell the truth.

Of telling a lie, my mother told me that people shouldn't lie because they will only end up having to cover their lies up by lying over and over again. She told me about someone she knew who constantly told lies. She said that a person like that can never be believed or trusted by people. To this day, I don't tell lies regardless of how boring the real story might be when compared to an exaggerated version that could easily and likely believably be created. I want to be trusted by people. If you get caught in a lie, strong chances are that the people you lie to won't believe you or trust you when you tell the truth. Additionally, it feels good to be a teller of the truth. Tell the truth.

## Chapter Twelve

Have hands-on experiences

A person's hands-on experiences throughout life are great ways for a person to learn. My father liked, while my mother insisted, that I try every opportunity that was available to me in school, in the community, and at church. My mother, in particular, said that if I didn't try many different activities, I would never know if I like them. Though there were times I could have logically felt overworked during my childhood, I now must admit once again that my mother was right. By trying practically every activity available to me, I learned what I liked and what I was good at, as well as what I didn't like and what I wasn't very good at doing. I liked some of the activities I was thrown into a great deal and disliked others an awful lot. The important thing was that at a young age, I was learning which activities I enjoyed being engaged in as well as those I was good at doing. Gratefully, I dropped the things that didn't mesh well with me, for one reason or another, without resistance.

During my childhood, I didn't worry about what I was doing or where I was going from day to day. I just knew that tomorrow would probably be another day when I'd be told get in the car because I needed to be somewhere. The destination of the drive would be to one of many activities. Incredibly, through my middle school years, I was involved with most every school sport for at least a short amount of time while exceling at none of them. I was a good bowler and a very good swimmer, but those were activities outside of school. In high school, I was on the golf team. Those activities taught me that I didn't like playing baseball and golf, likely because I was not good at playing either, nearly as much as doing other things. However, I have enjoyed watching others play baseball, and I still enjoy watching golf tournaments on television. The reason I enjoy watching these activities is likely because I experienced them somewhat.

By experiencing all of the activities I did during my youth, I learned a great deal about all of them as well as about myself. Positively, I also learned at an early age that I really enjoyed bowling, boxing, track-and-field activities, and especially swimming. Also, I didn't need to be pushed into doing anything related to music. That came naturally, and I enjoyed those activities immensely. Besides the school band, I enjoyed going to church and somewhat enjoyed singing in the youth choir with my older sister. If there were any spare minutes in the day, it was spent listening to music on the phonograph or on the radio. Also, I enjoyed being in the Cub Scouts, but I didn't like being in the Boy Scouts very much, probably because it wasn't all fun and games I enjoyed when I was a Cub Scout. Boy Scouts turned into a lot of time-consuming work that I had little time for since I was involved with so many other activities. Yet, I stayed in the Boy Scouts a long time because my dad really liked being involved with my Boy Scout troop. I didn't want to take that good-time activity away from him.

Besides so many organized activities, on the spur of the moment I would find myself sitting at a picnic table as a contestant in a pie-eating contest at summer community events my family attended. Pie, incidentally, is one of very few sweets I didn't like. There were many other times I suspect my mom was the one responsible for me ending up in other contests that involved eating, swimming, academics, music, and more. Many of the contests, like the pie-eating adventures, were obviously designed for the contestants to entertain the audience. As much as I loved to eat hot dogs and pizza pies, I don't remember ever winning any of those eating contests. Either I must have been a slow eater or just didn't want to win an eating contest for fear of getting teased about my weight and love of food. My weight already told me that I was a champ at eating. I didn't need a trophy to prove it to myself or anyone else. There were other contests that I won at times. In retrospect, I think my mom simply enjoyed thrusting me on stage so I'd have yet another life's experience in which I would continue to gain confidence by being in such a public situation and in which she could be proud of me. Then again, maybe there were times she just wanted me to be busy and out of her hair.

The point is that I had an incredible amount of experiences as I grew up. Mom was right. I was able to know through real-life experiences what I wanted to continue doing in life and what I wanted to cast aside. After having been exposed to such a life, I highly endorse experiencing all life has to offer at an early age. Furthermore, I applaud the parents who get their kids involved in a wide array of diverse activities including sports and music. It's a lot of work for a parent, but it does a child and his or her future a great amount of good.

Chapter Thirteen

Enjoy life's simple pleasures

Music is one of the greatest gifts a life can have. I know that music makes my life a whole lot better than it would be without it. Beyond having made music, which I increasingly so loved to do with my clarinet at a young age, I began to thoroughly enjoy listening to music more than doing any other leisurely activity. I got my first transistor radio and never, ever went anywhere without it, including the back seat of the family car as I would insist on sitting next to a window to get the best possible reception on the radio. Enjoy the simple pleasures in life, such as the joy of making and listening to music, because such pleasures can be the best things in life. Such a simple pleasure can be a needed friend when there is none around. It can change a mood when it needs to be changed for the better.

Remember to keep life's simple pleasures alive and well by obtaining them legally. If you basically steal them without paying for them, they may not be around forever. Here, I am talking about music. Help keep the simple pleasure of having great music in our lives by obtaining it legally so that the people who create the music get paid. Those who make the music that the world enjoys deserve to get paid for their efforts, time, and talents.

Other simple pleasures I've gotten to know during my life include reading and writing. I have spent a great deal of enjoyable time reading about music, politics, current events, and other topics that have enlightened or educated me at different periods throughout life. Since retiring from teaching, I have taken more time than I had allowed myself in the past to read current fiction writings. By doing so, I am sampling the types of stories publishers are accepting for publication and learning what readers are apparently enjoying. My reading experiences are an incentive for the fiction stories I am finally taking time to write during my semi-retirement years. In the process of reading and studying writing styles and scenarios, I have been very pleased to find that I love reading all kinds of fiction. Yet, I find it necessary to sometimes limit my reading and audio book listening time in order to have just as much time for another one of my simple pleasures, which is writing. As one can see by the writing of this book, I enjoy writing. Beyond enjoying to write about my opinions and my experiences, I like writing books with information about topics of which I am knowledgeable and interested. In recent times, I have begun writing stories of fiction, too. Fictional writing is something I have wanted to do for a long time and am finally taking time accomplish. The lesson to myself is that it is never too late to start something new.

Other simple pleasures I enjoy include dining out, visiting with friends, and taking short drives. Find the things you enjoy doing in life and treat yourself by taking time to do them. How I wish I would have taken more time to enjoy my passion for reading and writing through the years. Again, it's never too late to start. I have found that beyond enjoyable, taking time for one's simple pleasures is a good way to relax one's mind.

## Chapter Fourteen

Take time for God or another power every day

A person needs to make time to address whatever power he or she hopefully has in his or her life, the power that directs a person in a positive direction. I was confirmed at my family church at about this time in my life. Listing the presence of God in my life at a young age is appropriate and logical. Of all the things that come and go in life, God, or the other power one may choose, is an extremely positive constant. Even if it isn't praying every day or going to church weekly, let the thought of an Almighty One's power within you remain strong and present every day. Let this be in the good times as well as the bad. Faith gets one through the difficult times in life when challenges are faced whether those challenges are being entrenched in fear, grief, anger, or a combination of difficult emotions.

My belief has gotten me through challenging times. Ironically, it is during the most challenging times of life that I have become frustrated and even mad at God. Why did my father die at such a young age? Why did my sister have to suffer as she did with cancer and then pass away at an age that is considered way too young for these times? Such occurrences caused me to momentarily question a positive power because understanding such personal injustices was impossible. Yet, being guided into a strong religious life at an early age by my parents and holding on to such a life has helped me get through the bad times and has made me endlessly thankful for the good times. Additionally, believing in God and having the ultimate goal of getting to heaven helps a person choose those right paths instead of the wrong paths when traveling through life. I wish such a strong connection with a greater being for everyone as it is powerfully good.

## Chapter Fifteen

## Set goals

It is important for one to set goals. Just as importantly, it is important for one to make a plan as to how each goal will be achieved. Sometimes the timeline for reaching a goal is difficult to predict, but the method in which the goal will be achieved needs to be logically planned. For example, I may say I want to lose 20 pounds. While I can make a plan as to how I will exercise and diet to reach my goal, I may frustrate myself if I say I will lose that much weight in three months. In spite of my best efforts and my ability to follow my plan each day to lose the weight, my scale may not drop 20 pounds in three months. I have the goal and the plan to achieve it, but I don't set myself up for disappointment and failure by including a strict timeline within some of my goals.

Myself, I like to make New Year's resolutions. As long as I can remember, making New Year's resolutions has been an annual ritual for me. It all started at a very young age when my mother would ask me at the end of each year what my resolutions were for the New Year. There was no indication from her words or tone of voice that would make me even think of saying anything other than a detailed resolution. Quite commonly, the resolutions I'd make as a youngster would have to do with my school work or my clarinet playing. I could always say I would do better in school by studying more and by getting my homework finished, or I would resolve to spend more time practicing my clarinet. Those responses would almost satisfy my mother's question.

Yet, my mother would often suggest something like, "Why don't you also make a resolution to take out the garbage every Sunday night so it will ready for the garbage man on Monday morning?" After a pause, she would add, "Without me telling you to do it?" I'd grimace, shrug, and think that that would be a hard resolution to keep.

In time, the topic of making New Year's resolutions came up in school. To my surprise, I was one of very few students in the class who knew anything about New Year's resolutions. After the teacher explained it to the class, we were instructed to formally write our resolutions down on paper. We started each one with the words 'I resolve to…'

It wasn't until I was somewhat older that I would discuss New Year's resolutions with friends outside of school. I was surprised the first time someone told me, "I don't make them." I said, "I thought everybody made them." She protested, "Not me." Then she explained, "I'd only break them." As time went on, I surprisingly discovered that a lot of people don't make New Year's resolutions. I tried to promote the tradition when I taught school by making it a back-to-school writing assignment after the winter break ended in early January. As my teachers did in grade school, I had my students begin each resolution with the words "I resolve to…"

To this day, I believe in making New Year's resolutions and believe that making them is good for everyone. The way the process works, it can't be harmful to a person. First, as the end of the year approaches, it is logical to think of January 1 as a new beginning. It is also logical to think of the new beginning as a time one can improve himself or herself in some way. That's how I look at it. Personally, I find that resolutions slow the wild ride I sometimes take during the holiday period from Thanksgiving to the New Year, which possibly involve overeating, overspending, and doing other things that can't logically continue for health's sake or for my financial state's sake.

Admittedly, New Year's resolutions are difficult to keep. In time, I've learned to keep the list of resolutions short and detailed. Also, I've learned to make the resolutions reasonable so there's a good chance that I will successfully keep some of them the entire year and beyond. Honestly, though, if I keep one or two of the resolutions all year, I feel that I have been successful. I don't beat myself up over the resolutions I fail to keep. The reason is simple.

Let me explain with a recent year's New Year's resolutions. I resolved to lose some weight, to continue taking a lengthy walk every day, and to read the entire Bible. I also resolved to conquer some financial goals. By year's end, this was the breakdown. Every day of the year, I walked at least 15 minutes. Most days, I walked a longer amount of time, without stopping. As previously mentioned, I do my daily walks either on a treadmill, in a mall or huge store, or outdoors, which is my favorite place to walk. As can happen, there were a couple of days in which I didn't feel well enough to take my walk or had other pressing things to do; at those times, I would take two walks another day to make up for the lost walk. I made myself stick to the walking routine and am glad I did. It was a goal accomplished. My other successfully kept resolution was in reading the entire Bible within the year. I found a Bible app, which paced my reading of the Bible for 365 days. Throughout the year, there were times I was as much as two weeks ahead with my reading. A couple of times I got a couple of days behind. But, by year's end, I had read the entire Bible via the app. In fact, if memory serves me right, I finished that goal weeks before that year's end. Anyway, of that year's resolutions, those are the ones I kept. I walked and read the entire Bible.

My financial goals were unfortunately not met. I wasn't even close with that one. I had planned on having a good-sized savings account and some household purchases made by year's end. That year, unfortunately, I apparently liked spending money too much, and that goal didn't come to fruition. Though the resolution was doable, I failed. Subsequently, I chose to repeat that resolution, while knowing I would have to try harder in the future. On the positive side, though, during that particular calendar year, I curbed my spending for approximately the first six months with the resolution in my mind. Therefore, the failed resolution was better than not having any such resolution at all because I stuck to it for half of the year. That is obviously better than not watching my spending habits all 12 of the months of that year. My resolution to lose weight failed for the most part, too. However, I managed to lose some weight in the first four months of the year before that resolution went belly-up, pun intended. Again, the failed resolution was better than me having made no resolution regarding weight loss at all because I stuck to a diet plan for a third of the year, which is obviously better than not dieting all 12 months.

Make at least one resolution. Nobody has to know if you didn't stick to it all year. Even when you think you've failed, the time you've spent working on the resolution will have most likely done you some good. Again, even a failed resolution is better than having had no resolution at all. Also, of the resolutions that you succeed at, you may want to repeat them in order to continue improving yourself. For example, walking every day non-stop is a resolution I have enjoyed, for the most part, and I believe it has been good for me. Therefore, I have continued the walks via a new resolution every year since I first created the resolution years ago. The only thing I have changed is the length of time I require myself to walk. I continually increase the amount of time.

If you are still not convinced that New Year's resolutions are for you, it's not a problem. At least make goals for yourself, even if they aren't made at the beginning of a calendar's New Year. Each goal, naturally, should be designed to improve yourself. After all, everyone can change. If I didn't believe I could change, I probably would have died decades ago from the health problems that I sensed were creeping up on me from smoking too many cigarettes. If I didn't believe I could change, I would still be over 250 pounds and have never gotten my weight down to 200 pounds, give or take a few pounds. Granted, I still want to lose more weight. Anyway, I am proof that setting challenging goals can improve one's life when one stays focused on the goals and meets the goals. The older I get, the more I focus on either maintaining or improving my health. Naturally, I want to thrive physically as well as mentally for as long as I can.

I thoroughly enjoy reading about successful people to learn about where they started, where they traveled through life, and how they achieved their successful outcomes. Of the many successful people I have read about in history, whether they are in politics, business, entertainment, music, or another line of work, they all have one common characteristic. Successful people have had goals. They had a burning desire to achieve their goals before they became successful. Another glaring characteristic that I have noticed about successful people is that they don't necessarily compete with other people. Many successful persons have set stringent goals for themselves and have only competed with themselves to achieve their best results. Therefore, it isn't necessary to defeat or ruin others to meet your goals. Concentrate on yourself, and consider only competing with yourself to get the best out of you.

Likewise, being a smart person is really overrated. There are many smart people who procrastinate and never accomplish much of anything. They don't set goals or focus on achieving results. Regardless of intelligence, successful people have set goals for themselves and have focused on those goals so that they eventually complete their tasks. At the end of the day, they have something to show to themselves for their existence. Set goals for yourself. Go after the impossible dream you have within yourself while competing with your best performance to date.

Finally, about setting goals, time your goals properly. Lack of success in achieving goals may have to do with the timing one places on trying to achieve something in life. Beyond what was mentioned in another chapter's discussion about patience, some things in life may not only take time to be achieved, but they may take proper timing in which goals may be successfully achieved as well. Logically plan the best time of life to achieve your goals. Depending on the goal one plans to achieve, there may very well be a time that is too early in life or too late in life for obtaining the best possible results in achieving a goal. In other words, rushing into something can be as unproductive as procrastinating. Proper timing is important.

Though this chapter is specifically about the importance of setting goals, goals are repeatedly mentioned throughout the life's lessons promoted in this book. Besides mentioning one's goal or goals in this chapter of this book, the word 'goal' also appears in the introduction, the conclusion, as well as in eleven other chapters. Setting goals has been an important element leading to the successes throughout my life. Therefore, to others, I highly recommend the practice of setting goals.

## Chapter Sixteen

Keep a calendar

At a relatively young age, I started writing the events that were important to me on a calendar that I kept in the nightstand by my bed. I was always somewhat of a worrier about forgetting things such as someone's birthday or my parent's anniversary. I thought it would be disrespectful to forget such events. I highly recommend that everyone honor others who are important in their lives by remembering such important dates as well. Naturally, keeping the calendar updated with important events you need to remember to attend, such as professional or job-related meetings, is important, too. Though current technology devices make it easy for many businesses, such as doctor and dentist offices, to remind people of their appointments, it is a good idea to keep such appointments listed in one's calendar as well.

Of the personal life reminders, it can include birthdays of relatives and close friends. When one is busy, it is easy to forget a day or an event that can respectfully be remembered via different methods. In current times, one can set reminders via electronic gadgets to get notified of the important dates and events just before they occur. Depending on the device used, the device can be set to send a reminder minutes, hours, days, or even a week before the important time occurs. In fact, reminders can come more than once, such as a week before an event so that you can prepare for it and then again the day before the event so that you remember to attend it. Of course, after the reminders arrive, act on them.

Back in the day, I had a reputation for being one who always remembered other people's important days. In recent times, it isn't as unique because people are reminded of birthdays, anniversaries, and other special days and events by simply opening Facebook where people post such information. People likely appreciate being remembered on their important days, and it is an excellent way to let people know that they are important or even special to you.

Before the calendars were available on computers, I'd document events 5 to 7 days in advance in order to drop a birthday card or anniversary card in the mail. In current times, a reminder given just a day or two before an event is a sufficient amount of time for scheduling an e-card or to shop for a gift that will be delivered by hand, if the relationship warrants it. Of course, there are still times I do the old-school method of mailing a card. Those cards are really appreciated nowadays as many people do not mail cards. As one friend told me a couple of years ago with delight in his voice, "You're the only one who still mails me a birthday card."

The events and dates that one can document is limitless, obviously. I have used the calendar with reminder options for important dates of family members, a small circle of close friends, and anyone I might want to please or impress. When I taught full-time, I also made notations of such events as secretary's day, boss' day, and the dates by which I needed to buy treats for my students prior to holidays, which is something I did practically each year that I taught. Whether written or technological, calendars are easy to use and worth the effort. Besides making you feel good about yourself for remembering others, the people you remember will appreciate your thoughtfulness.

# Chapter Seventeen

## Don't show that you're upset

Assuming everyone gets upset at times, it is often best not to show that you are bothered by someone else's words or actions. After all, it could be that someone's words came out wrong or actions were miscommunicated, and the person didn't mean to upset you. By not reacting, if a person's words or actions were simply a case of miscommunication, you are graciously giving the person a way out of an uncomfortable situation. Of course, if you are the one who unintentionally hurt or upset someone with your words or actions, it is most appropriate for you to say, "I'm sorry. That came out wrong." Possibly, you could admit, "I'm sorry. I didn't mean to do that." Hopefully another would deliver the same messages to you if he or she unintentionally upset you.

On the other hand, if you believe a person said something hurtful to you with the purpose of upsetting you, it is still often best not to show that you're upset. Just like when being bullied, don't give anyone the satisfaction of letting him or her think or even know that he or she upset you. After all, if the person is vindictive, the person's goal is to get you to feel bad. That is identical to a bully's goal when victimizing a person. In many situations, if you show no negative reaction to being treated hurtfully, you are showing the person who is attempting to upset you that he or she is not going to get any satisfaction out of treating you badly because you refuse to reveal that you are hurt by it. It's best not to give the person who is trying to upset you the awkward and desired reward of upsetting you.

This does not mean that you shouldn't respond to the person's words. It just means that, if you became upset, you do not need to show it. You might even go as far as letting the person know that you are aware that he or she is trying to upset you by saying, "You are trying to get me upset. Please, explain why." Considering the person, you might not want to take the high road, as they say, and be more blatantly rude yourself by saying, "If you want to get me upset, you're going to have to try harder than that. Truth be told, I don't get upset very easily. My advice to you is to just save your breath." You have a right to respond on equal terms when a person is obviously trying to upset you, put you down, or insult you with rude words or actions.

Another approach to cut off a person who is trying to unnecessarily upset you is to stand up for yourself by saying, "You can stop trying to upset me because I don't care what you think (about me or this situation)." If the person persists, reiterate: "Like I said, your negative opinion (of me or this situation) isn't important to me. So let's talk about something else." If the person persists, you should have no hesitation about saying good-bye to the person and calmly walking away. In summation, no one has the right to rudely upset you, so don't give anyone the satisfaction in thinking they have successfully done so. Remember, people treat you the way you allow them to treat you. When someone oversteps his or her bounds by becoming unnecessarily rude, state your dissatisfaction without getting upset or without showing you are upset. If the person refuses to stop the behavior, calmly excuse yourself and move on.

## Chapter Eighteen

Trust mom's advice

When you need guidance early in life, trust in your mother's advice or the advice of someone else you trust. If not mom's, try another adult of whom you've grown to know and respectfully trust through time. Your personal advisor can be anyone who you sincerely feel has your best interest at heart. The person could be your mom, dad, spouse, another relative, a friend, a professional counselor, or a respected figure in your church. It can be anyone who you strongly feel will help you during your times of indecision. My mom and dad strongly advised that I start looking for a college to attend so that I could continue my education after I graduate from high school. Like many teens back in the 1960s, I had the option of continuing my education and accumulating some debt at a young age or just going out and getting a job to earn some money after graduating from high school. While acting like there was no decision to be made on the issue, my mom provided constant guidance, or perhaps pressure, by having me apply to colleges during my last year-and-a-half of high school. Though I sometimes wanted to stray from the path laid out for me by my parents, I trusted them as advisors. I will always be thankful for the wise advice they strongly gave and I ultimately accepted.

Through the years when I had important decisions to make, I naturally made the final decisions on my own. Yet, there were times I wanted to hear what someone else might do if they were in my position. While getting the advice of co-workers, friends, or other relatives was interesting and sometimes helpful or reassuring, I found that the most satisfying advice came from my most trusted advisors in my youth, my parents. During the very important decision-making years that occur early in life, trust your parents who are most likely the people who know you best and who care about you the most.

Chapter Nineteen

Document practically everything

Take notes and document anything that you need to remember or that is worth remembering. Definitely keep some sort of documented diary during the important travels in your life. When I was 18 years old, I did absolutely none of this recordkeeping when I had what may very well end up being the travel experience of my life. I spent a month in Europe. In my last year of high school, I was selected as the second chair clarinetist in the School Band of America and traveled throughout Europe for 28 days. Of that whirlwind band and orchestra tour, I remember some of it but not a great deal, including where I had different experiences. The band moved so quickly from one place to another that I scarcely had time to scribble down as much as a note about my travels. It's hard to believe that I took this trip without a camera. Of course, this trip occurred approximately a half-century ago when phones with cameras did not exist. In fact, cameras were not very commonplace.

In retrospect, my lack of taking notes has become somewhat devastating as it has been difficult through the years for me to talk about the trip. Furthermore, I am unable to even relive the adventures in my mind because the details have faded in time. All I remember is that I was terribly homesick during the first couple days of the trip as it was my first time away from home for an extended period of time. After the first few days, however, I was so busy and was having such a great time that taking a few minutes a day to take notes didn't even cross my mind. Even though my mom gave me a little diary to write notes throughout the month, the diary ended up in the bottom of my suitcase and was completely forgotten about. Literally, within days after getting back home from the trip, I was off to college and didn't take time to document the trip then either. Sadly, there is no timely documentation of my personal trip of my lifetime.

As it turned out, I have not been much of a traveler throughout my life, and memories provided by notes of that incredible excursion would have done me quite well. The lesson I learned was to take notes during the very important times in life. There will likely be times in the future when one will want to relive memories and share them with others, either verbally or in writing. Documenting will make it possible.

Beyond suggesting that one take notes during his or her major events in life, I recommend taking notes in the simplest of situations, too, for the remembrance factor. I have always encouraged my students in my classrooms through the years to take notes. Though a person thinks they will remember something, sometimes memory fails. Additionally, when learning something, one may think that one point or another in a lesson isn't important, but then he or she finds that it would be good to know sometime in the future. Having the advantage of looking back at one's notes can save time and effort in the future.

Lastly, writing something down can help people remember information. When I had students correctly write the spelling words they missed on a test a number of times, I explained that writing something down does help a person remember. My example to adult students was to ask them, "How many times have you made a grocery list and then didn't need to even look at it when you got to the grocery store?" My point is obvious. When a person writes something down, he or she remembers it longer. Again, a person should document throughout life. It can help a person a great deal.

## Chapter Twenty

Speak well

To make a good impression on people, it is important that one learn to speak well. Knowing proper grammar and developing a good vocabulary will assist a person in coming across better than he or she would otherwise. A person sounds educated and generally intelligent when speaking well. As for the content delivered when one speaks, thought should precede the words spoken. One should be informed with the latest information so he or she is accurately correct with spoken messages. Remember the advice President Abraham Lincoln gave about speaking. He said, "Better to remain silent and be thought a fool than to speak out and remove all doubt."

If it is a presentation or a speech that is being given, be prepared before speaking. Time permitted, practice delivering words. While one shouldn't read his or her words, having notes is good for making sure one remembers to say everything one had planned to say. Additionally, notes assist a person in delivering a message's content in a logical order. Naturally, a talk with content that logically flows is easier for listeners to comprehend than a disjointed delivery. Again, if possible, do not read to an audience as it makes the speaker appear to be less prepared and much less confident. Depending on the circumstances of a speech or presentation, some may interpret being read to as a lack of respect for an audience, as well.

Naturally, one should speak clearly with proper volume and enunciation. If one doesn't, the purpose of speaking to communicate may be defeated because the message being delivered may not be heard or understood by every listener. Depending on the venue for speaking, a microphone with accompanying speakers may be offered to a speaker. Use the microphone. It is there for a purpose. A speaker never knows how difficult it may be for some people in the audience to hear him or her in different areas of a room or how difficult it is for some members of an audience to hear in general. In particular, speak loudly and clearly when speaking to a mature audience, which may have persons who have great difficulty hearing due to their ages.

When speaking, rather than getting frustrated with people who say they don't understand or are unable to hear you, change the way you deliver your words. If you stubbornly refuse to change your delivery so that others can hear and understand you, it won't change the fact that people do not understand or hear you. Respond to complaints in which others say they are having difficulty with hearing or understanding you by altering how you are delivering your words.

I was attending a meeting in a large room in which microphones were provided to a panel of speakers. One speaker refused to turn his microphone on and pull it closer to himself. Instead, he shouted to the audience, "If you can't hear me, you need a Beltone!" A Beltone, incidentally, is the name brand of a hearing aid. After shouting that, he spoke softer and softer and softer. When people started complaining that he couldn't be heard, by either stating so or by gesturing with cupped hands behind their ears, he started shouting again rather than using the microphone. Beyond not sounding pleasant as he delivered his partially shouted and mostly unheard message, he looked like a disrespectful fool for not using his provided microphone as all the other speakers were doing. Don't be insulted or oddly uncooperative when asked to speak up or to use a microphone.

In conversation, stifle the awkward and annoying 'umm' and be generous with the words and phrases 'please,' 'thank you,' and 'you're welcome.' Additionally, when having a conversation, speak 'with' people and not 'to' them. Speaking 'to' a person can be construed by the listener as being talked down to and being treated disrespectfully. Remember to keep a substantial amount of eye contact during a conversation. Some etiquette experts say that 70 percent of eye contact during conversation is appropriate. Others say substantially less eye contact is fine. However, if you give much more than 70 percent eye contact during a lengthy conversation, you can come across as being intimidating. Contrarily, if your eye contact is far too little, you may be perceived as disinterested or bored with the conversation. Also, be aware of your voice's tone and quality by making it appropriate for the situation. One should avoid talking in a monotone, as it is annoying to the listener and can easily distract a person from your content. Some people totally tune out a person who speaks in a monotone.

It is best to not curse, unless you know the loose language will not offend the people with whom you are speaking. If you curse, do so sparingly so it will have the intended impact you want it to have on your verbal message. This, of course, is not a suggestion one needs to follow when they are speaking loosely around friends who won't judge by the use of one's foul language. Some people consider cursing to be disrespectful and may tune you out if you engage in such language. My advice is for a speaker to not swear when the speaker is unfamiliar with the audience or has a large audience. The odds are that some persons in a large audience are offended by cursing.

Also, if everyone present speaks one language, be sure to speak in the language that is common to all. Don't isolate people by speaking in a foreign language that only some people in the audience understand. I had a superior on a job who sometimes spoke Spanish to her Hispanic secretary when others who were present only spoke English. It appeared to be no less rude to the non-Spanish speakers than had the superior whispering in her secretary's ear in front of everyone. Beyond rude, it appeared ignorantly awkward that the superior wouldn't simply take the secretary into her nearby office and talk privately if she didn't want others to know what she was telling her secretary.

Lastly, on the topic of speaking well, don't correct another person's incorrect grammar or wrong word choices unless you have a right to discreetly correct him or her. You more likely have a right to correct a person if you are the person's teacher, parent, or a friend who is close enough to the person to make constructive corrections.

Naturally, the corrections should be made privately and not in front of others to avoid embarrassment to the speaker. Without alleged permission to correct a person's spoken errors involving grammar, word pronunciation, or incorrect word usage, the person who corrects the speaker publicly can be seen as a snobby know-it-all, which may likely be considered worse than not speaking well. Lastly, on correcting people's speech, make sure you are correct before correcting someone.

The reason I chose this year to include speaking well is because I became quite aware of how I presented myself when I spoke during my first college speech course. After I gave my first speech in the class, the notes from the teacher let me know that I was doing things wrong that I had never even realized. I was surprised at his comment that read, "You say the word 'get' with a short i sound instead of a short e sound." I never realized I was doing that until then. Later in the course, he suggested that I work at projecting my voice more so that I could be heard more easily. Additionally, the teacher probably wanted me to appear more self-confident when speaking before a large group. All in all, one should make a conscious effort to speak well. Speaking well not only does a speaker a great deal of good, but it can give more satisfaction to his or her listeners, too.

## Chapter Twenty-One

## Realize the importance of family

More than realizing the importance of family, express it. Tell family members how much they mean to you, if they are important to you. Do this not only for them but for yourself as well. I lost my father during my third year of college, and there have been so many things that I wish I would have told him. Most of all, if he had lived longer, I would have told him how very much he meant to me and how much I appreciated him. Beyond that, there are so many things I would have asked my father that must now go unanswered.

I was concerned about my lack of having told my father how important he was in my life and my lack of not having verbally expressed more fully how much I loved him. I felt I had never told him assertively enough as to how much I appreciated all he had done for me, the family, and so many other people. I was so proud of him but I do not remember verbalizing it. When I expressed these inner disappointments in myself to my mother, it was the first time I remember ever having cried beyond childhood tears. She graciously guaranteed me that my father definitely knew how much I loved him and how much I appreciated and respected him. For that, I have always been grateful to her. After all, she knew my father better than anyone else and she would have known that about him. Yet, carrying that feeling of inadequacy in myself after my father's death, I made sure I didn't make the same mistake with my mother and others as I often told them and showed them how important they were in my life, how grateful I was for their constant support in everything I tried to accomplish in life, and how much I loved them.

Even if you think family or anyone else knows how much they mean to you, make sure they know. Tell them. Show them. It not only will be important and satisfying to them, but it will give you satisfaction as well.

## Chapter Twenty-Two

Be yourself

You don't have to be like everybody else. Lord knows I'm not like the norm of society in every way. At times, I'm glad I'm not. By the grace of God and common sense, I have learned that I do not have to be like everyone else, even if it means I don't always feel like I fit in. A very minor example of feeling different was when I turned 21 in 1971 during my third year of college. It wasn't until then that I had my first beer. Just from the smell of it, which I never liked, I knew I could easily wait to try drinking it. As it turned out, my mother bought me my first beer on my 21st birthday. She insisted that we go out to eat and have a drink on the milestone event in an effort to act as if everything was getting back to normal even though it was an excruciatingly sad time for the family. This overly-hyped birthday arrived just a month and four days after my father had suddenly and shocking passed away from a heart attack at the young age of 52. As we sat at Lums Restaurant, which sadly closed decades ago in our area, little did my mother probably know or little would she probably even believe that the beer she ordered for me was my first beer.

I hated it. I didn't tell her at the time, but as I slowly downed the big glass of foaming beer, I was very disappointed in the taste. Actually, the foam was interesting and not bad, but the 90% or more of the glass that was liquid tasted as nasty to me as it smelled. The meal that was to come couldn't come fast enough to replace the taste in my mouth. Yet, I kept my secret of hating beer for a long time. In time, my detestation for beer became obvious when I was out with friends. Yes, I was a college guy who hated beer. How awkward was that? Though I had contemplated nursing one beer all night in an effort to hide the fact that I didn't like beer, I didn't do it. Instead, I'd have sodas, or pop as we call it in the Midwest. I still drink pop instead of beer the times I'm in such a setting. While the fact that I don't like to drink beer still raises eyebrows in some circles, those circles can just keep spinning.

Of course, this is just one small example of the ways in which I found I was different from most other people. Each time, I survived the social consequences regardless of how uncomfortable others would sometimes try to make me feel about being different. When I find I'm unique or different from most people, I have been fairly comfortable living with the uniqueness. Furthermore, when I am different than the norm, I am different without coming across as though I am trying to prove something to others. Some people feel a need to prove themselves for some reason and end up being an irritant. The number of times I had to refrain from saying to others, "You want me to drink, and you need to stop." I just bite my tongue, so to speak, and keep the thought to myself. I remember one time in particular when a former college roommate organized a group to meet at a bowling alley. One of the men that I hardly knew at the gathering got more and more inebriated as the night went on. He singled me out for being a non-drinker and insisted that I drink and loosen up. There was another non-drinker in the group who he didn't harass. Again, I was asking myself, "Why me, Lord?" The drunker the heavy drinker became, the more he pestered me to drink. Out of respect to the rest of the people in the group, I didn't cause a scene even though I felt I had every right to do so. Apparently, the patience I had learned years ago was being engaged.

Beyond the beer, there are other situations where I am not in with the alleged in-crowd. I am often left out of conversations about television shows because I generally don't like to watch television. I had given it enough of a chance early in my life, but since I was a teenager, I just don't enjoy spending my free time watching television. A fellow teacher at a school I worked at was in the faculty lunch room talking about a television show. As I likely showed incredible disinterest, she turned to me as she was talking to the small group and asked me, "You do watch 'Friends,' don't you?" I said, "No." She raised her voice in disbelief: "You never watched 'Friends?'" I repeated, "No," as she continued looking at me in disbelief. There were likely eyes rolling in the room as if to say 'I told you he was weird!'

If I'm near a television, I watch the local news if it's time for it to come on. On a lazy weekend afternoon, if I am tired and just want to lie on the sofa and turn on the television rather than sleep, I occasionally find myself going through the channels and stopping on either golf or boxing. These aren't programs I go out of my way to fit in my schedule, but if I run into them, I watch them. It is somewhat odd that I enjoy watching golf since I haven't ever enjoyed doing it. Also, I have taped the game show 'Jeopardy' and select award shows like the Grammys and Oscars. Sometimes I watch the recordings, but more often I don't. At times I have gotten so backed up with the unviewed programs that I have deleting many at once. However, when that extremely rare mood strikes and I want to watch something, I have enough episodes of 'Jeopardy' and award shows saved up to spend time experiencing what it is like to be a couch potato.

I have preferred listening to the latest news, talk shows, or music on the radio while I'm driving in my car. If that doesn't appeal to me at the moment, I always have an audio-book or two from the library available to me. I find current events, politics, the day's local news stories, fiction audio-books, or various types of music to be more entertaining and interesting than most any of the so-called entertainment programs available on television in recent times. When there is a buzz about one television show or another, I sometimes tape it, give it a chance, and end up still believing that watching television programs isn't how I want to spend my time. Having people consider me to be different for not liking television is not a concern for me.

People are also somewhat shocked when I say that I, who was a teenager in the 1960s, never engaged in illegal drugs. Back in the day, the closest I came to trying illegal drugs was when I was with a friend at a night club in the early 1970s. He wanted to go outside to get some fresh air, and we started walking around the building that was on the near North Side of Chicago. When we were in the alley behind the club, he reached into his jacket and said in a quiet voice, "Look what I got today." He took out a marijuana cigarette, which was called a joint back then, and he lit it up. He shoved it towards me and said, "Have some." I took my cigarette out of my mouth and put the joint to my lips. Then I asked myself why I was doing this. I stopped short of taking any. Unlike former President Bill Clinton, I not only didn't inhale, I didn't even puff on it. I reasoned that I was about a 45-minute drive from home, if I drove the speed limit, and I wouldn't know what affect it would have on me since I had never experienced it before. So, my first opportunity to try it back in the day was passed on. It wouldn't be long after that when I had more opportunities to partake in using drugs. My second blatant opportunity was when a teacher who taught with me invited me to her apartment to smoke some weed after school one day. She said others would be there as well. I passed. I later found out that one of the pot-smokers was someone who eventually became a school administrator. While it wouldn't be surprising to me now, it was to me back then. Though I had been curious about the effects that drugs would have on me, the curiosity never got the best of me. As I said, this shocks some people because I don't really think I appear to be all that incredibly uncool. Honestly, the legality of it all has had impact on me. Incidentally, marijuana is legal in Illinois as of January 1, 2020. Therefore, by the time readers are reading this book in 2020 or later, I can try marijuana legally in my locality if I so desire. While I have not been proud of being what many would call uncool, regarding drug usage, I am proud of my ability to refrain by having said no to drugs regarding legality's sake.

Beyond beer, television, and illegal drugs, I tend to be unique among my family and friends in not liking to try different foods. As I recall, the last new food I was talked into trying was sushi. I had to grab a napkin to discretely spit it out. When I'm not dieting, I love to eat deep dish Chicago-style pizzas with no more than cheese and sausage on a scrumptious butter crust like Lou Malnati's Pizzeria serves and cheese hot dogs on a bun with mustard and relish. I also love spaghetti with sausage and lots of American cheese if it's made incredibly well like Mom used to make. Depending on the strictness of the latest diet I am on, I also love roasted barbecue chicken with stuffing, a baked potato, and a side salad with ranch or Thousand Island dressing just like many Midwest restaurants commonly serve. When in a breakfast mood, which isn't very often, I like American cheese omelets with buttered wheat toast and hash brown potatoes. In the dessert department, most any chocolate concoction put in front of me disappears in record-time. Whether it is milk chocolate or dark chocolate doesn't matter. I love chocolate. That, literally, is about all I really, really like to eat. As you are probably thinking, based on my favorite foods, the bathroom scale has never been a good friend of mine.

An update since the first edition of this book, which was written approximately five years ago in 2015, is that I began a low carb-high protein diet and lost about ten pounds in 2018. Not being satisfied with the small weight loss after several months, I transitioned to the Keto diet in late 2018. Within approximately a half of a year, I lost another 30 pounds. In the past several months, the scale does not decline in numbers anymore. Therefore, in spite of still seeing myself as a dieter, I am stuck at 40 pounds down as of the writing of this book. As any dieter can imagine, I'm sure, it takes incredible willpower to continue dieting on a diet that is not showing results anymore, or I need to find another diet to get down to my desired weight.

Continuing with this life's lesson about one's uniqueness being okay, I was unique back in the day was my preference to be single. As the years progress, remaining single is not considered nearly as unusual as it used to be. There are more and more people choosing to be single whether it is by never having been married or by getting divorced. When eyebrows were raised over my being single in the past, I have simply stated the truth in an effort to lower the eyebrows. I admitted that I never met anyone with whom I would want to spend the rest of my life. Of the times I thought I may have met someone with whom I wanted to spend the rest of my life, I later found that I was wrong.

Forcing acceptance of your uniqueness on others can be frustrating for them. When others tell me of their uniqueness, which are often idiosyncrasies, they give information about themselves that they could just as well have left out of a conversation. They specifically need to leave some of their idiosyncrasies to themselves if their purpose of sharing is to get others to accept their oddities. Besides, a little mystery or unknown details about a person is often more interesting than the idiosyncrasies some people share about themselves. My advice is that one should keep people guessing about some aspects of his or her life by not divulging everything. A little intrigue about yourself may keep others more interested in you and keep them coming back in an effort to learn more about you.

While asserting that it may be smart for you to keep some of your uniqueness private, don't be overly secretive, either. You don't want to appear so private that it looks like you have something to hide, either. There's a medium here. Also, when being different, be careful not to be different simply for argument's sake as some people apparently do to get attention. There are many times a person fits in well by conforming, if it is something they can comfortably do. Look at it this way. There are times it takes courage to step out of the norm just as it might take courage for a person to conform. The beauty of it all is that one has the freedom to choose how and when to go rogue and when to conform. Whether going rogue or conforming, do what keeps you honest with yourself and hopefully comfortable with yourself. After all, the one person you have to live with is yourself.

Chapter Twenty-Three

Teach the children well

In this entry, I offer my top ten lessons that children should be taught, as well as talk about how teachers should interact with children properly for a child to best succeed in school and in life. I feel I know this because it was in the classroom where I spent much of my life interacting with young people. Having dealt with young people for 33 years in public schools and with young family members since I was in college when my sister's children were born, I feel right in offering my top ten lessons, which I believe children should be taught by their parents and others who interact with them during their developmental years. Therefore, I begin this entry with ten lessons I believe children can benefit from being taught.

1. Respect elders. Children should be taught to respect everyone. In particular, however, they should be taught to respect elders as it does not appear to be something that comes naturally to some of them. Stress to children that everyone should respect the generations of persons who are older than their own generation and explain the reasons why. First and foremost, people who are older have obviously done some things right to reach the age they have achieved. They are survivors. By having been around longer, they have had more experiences, and some of those experiences will never be had by people again because the older people lived in a time when life was much different than it is today. Encourage children to understand this and to interact positively with older people so that they can learn from their elders. Otherwise, the day will come when the older people they know aren't in their lives anymore and the younger people will regret not having learned all they could have learned and benefitted from them.

It's sad to see how many elders are ignored by younger persons. Unfortunately, I have personally experienced it. It's extremely frustrating to hear younger persons assert themselves as though they know more or know better than an older person and then say something like, "That was then – this is now!" For example, one young relative told me when I was deep in a nonsensical political debate with him, "Oh, so you're going to throw your age in my face." Those younger people need to be taught early in life that every new generation can learn from the past. Needless to say, that is why it is so important that history be taught and learned. Studying history, among people and among nations, is essential so that past mistakes are not repeated. Again, respecting elders as well as interacting with elders is an extremely important lesson that should be instilled in a child's upbringing. When a child learns to respect elders, the lesson will hopefully extend to his or her respect being given to all people.

2. Know God. Beyond knowing God, fear God or a supreme being who is introduced to children by family early in life. Think of the times that the fear of God kept you from doing something you shouldn't do. Children may need that extra incentive to stop them when considering doing wrong. Children may need the love of God to keep them doing what is right and best for them throughout lifetime. Youngsters deserve to have the fear-of-God advantage as well as the love of God advantage in their lives. Beyond making a person the best person he or she can be, it may be a person's lifesaver someday.

3. Respect yourself and take care of yourself. Children need to learn that being safe is primarily their responsibility because, logically, every individual is the only one who is with himself or herself all the time. If someone should ever ask a child to do something that doesn't seem right, the child should know not to do it. A child needs to learn that, unfortunately, there are bad people in the world who don't respect other people. Therefore, children should not do anything that is disrespectful or potentially harmful to themselves when told to do something that isn't right. It's not as easy as teaching a child to not talk to strangers. After all, not talking to strangers is a rule that may best be broken when a youngers is in

need; it depends on the difficult situation of which a child may be engaged. Being too skeptical can sometimes be as detrimental as being too trusting. At an early age, children need to practice deciphering between right and wrong as well as deciphering between the good and bad in people. This is easier said than done, as many of life's rules are. Yet, experience and practice in dealing with people will get children on the right path to protecting themselves from evils that may lurk.

4. Work hard. Teach children that by working hard they have the best opportunity of obtaining the most and the best that life has to offer them. A good place to start instilling this lesson in children is by teaching them to work hard in school. It's the first structured experience they will likely have that is similar to their eventual jobs and tasks later in life. More than the material things that they can acquire from working hard to earn a decent paycheck later in life, working hard will garner self-respect and cherished respect from others.

5. Life won't always seem fair. Children need to learn how to cope with the reality that life isn't always fair. This lesson encompasses learning to deal with inevitable frustrations, disappointments, and failures. Children need to be forewarned that life won't always be what they envision to be fair. They should understand that it is simply an unfortunate part of living. Let them know that they aren't alone in feeling life isn't fair at times because everyone has the same feeling from time to time. In an effort to counteract times of disappointment, remind them that there should be times when life is quite good and more than fair.

6. Be honest. Be honest even when it is difficult to do so. Being honest encompasses keeping one's promise to others. Children ought to be taught early that liars are rarely trusted and can have a very difficult time in developing strong relationships. To become a person who is trusted by others and a person who others will want to have as a friend, be honest. Not being honest can cause many problems in one's life, including the dislike of one's self.

7. Consider the feelings of other people. Being honest does not mean that you need to be so blunt that you ignore that people's feelings can be hurt. There are definitely times you can simply not speak rather than be so blatantly honest that you offend people and make them feel bad. Another way of saying this is to let children know that they should not be mean to others and, when possible, should avoid making people feel bad. This lesson goes along with the assertion that one should treat others the way he or she wants to be treated.

8. Don't waste things. Regardless of whether it is one's abilities, emotions, food, money, toys, time, relationships, or anything else, the sooner a child learns not to waste anything, the better off he or she will be.

9. Be tolerant and non-judgmental of others. No two people are exactly the same. As children begin to realize that people are different, they need to learn to respect people who are different than they are. They need to be taught to accept others as their equal. Additionally, no one is perfect. When others make unintentional mistakes, children need to understand that everyone errs, and forgiving people is just. The good thing in making a mistake, it should be taught, is that one can learn from mistakes.

10. Keep your germs to yourself and avoid getting other people's germs. Primarily, cover your sneezes and coughs. Also, keep a distance from those who don't practice this rule. Obviously, teaching children not to spread their germs by covering their mouth when coughing or sneezing is also part of showing respect for others. This rule can easily extend into other common sense practices involving healthy living with appropriate hygiene practices, which everyone should maintain throughout life.

In conclusion to the list of lessons children should be taught, remember that children may be influenced more by what they see rather than what they are told, much as an adult is often more impacted by another person's actions rather than one's words. For the best developments in children, set good examples through your actions and interactions with them. Yet, one of the lessons that should be exemplified for a child is the art of listening. When a child speaks, an adult needs to listen undistractedly to the child. Respectfully allow a child the opportunity to have his or her say. Then, after he or she has spoken on anything of which a response is logically appropriate, the adult should then express himself or herself with the child being instructed to listen. The importance of respectful reciprocation in speaking and listening with another person leads to better communications with and relationships with others throughout life.

\*\*\*

Beyond the lessons that need to be taught to youngsters, I have strong opinions about how teachers should interact with children. This is where I have expertise through my experiences and education. After I graduated from college at 22 years of age, I started teaching with the notion that I would just give it a try. I didn't expect too much of myself in terms of turning teaching into a life-long career because I didn't enjoy student teaching during my senior year in college. Besides that, I spent all four years of my college life working at the college radio station as an on-air disc jockey while also being the station manager during the last two years of the four-year radio engagement. At the time, radio work was all I wanted to do for the rest of my life, as unrealistic as that desire may have been. Being an on-air radio personality is one of those jobs that too many people want and therefore many rarely get. The supply and demand is way out of proportion for persons seeking radio jobs. Like me, they want to get paid for allegedly having all that fun. Though I dreamed a long time about such a full-time job being given to me one day, it didn't happened. During one interview after graduating from college, I was thrust on the air and thought I did a good job. However, the program director spoke to me after my airtime and felt differently. He said that I blew it when I said before a commercial, "And now a word of interest." He said, "Everybody hates commercials. They aren't interesting." All of a sudden, radio and the critical people behind the scenes didn't seem like they were going to be much fun to work for after all. The truth is that I had very little experience with commercials because college radio doesn't air commercials. Anyway, I worked part-time for several years at three different professional radio stations during my college years as well as for several years after I graduated, when I had started my teaching career. The dream radio job, especially with its extremely low pay in the small radio markets, never became a full-time reality for me. To my delight, teaching quickly turned into a job that I wanted to continue doing, and the intended short-term teaching profession became a career that lasted more than four decades. Thirty-three of those years were spent teaching children full-time and that was followed by seven-and-a-half years of teaching adults in part-time teaching jobs at community colleges.

Of the few disappointments I found in teaching, the biggest ones involved the conduct of some teachers. I saw teachers wanting to be the students' friends instead of their disciplinarian and a positive role model for their students. Fortunately, there weren't many teachers like that, but there should have been none. I was very popular when I started teaching as I found that students tend to really like many young teachers. That doesn't mean, however, that I went out of my way to be overly friendly with them or that I didn't discipline them firmly when I needed to do so. As I continued my teaching career, naturally I became older and saw younger teachers enter the profession. Like me, many of them were popular with the students, too. The problem was that some of these young teachers seemed to enjoy being popular with the students too much, and they failed to discipline as necessary, perhaps for fear that they would lose popularity with their students. Furthermore, I found that some of the young teachers entering the profession just didn't know how to discipline. It was a part of teaching that wasn't always taught back in the day.

Any teacher who has had to work with another teacher who has wanted students to be his or her friend more than anything else makes teaching incredibly difficult for the other educators at the school. What happens is that the students resent that there are teachers who make them behave and do their schoolwork when they see other teachers who are bending over backwards to be well-liked by the students and letting them get away with their poor behaviors and not having to work diligently in school. When it comes to teaching children, one should teach them well while incorporating discipline. One who enters the teaching profession must make teaching his students right from wrong a primary responsibility.

Anyone who wants to be the kids' best friend should find another line of work such as being a party host at an entertainment facility or taking a job that requires no more than supervisory duties for keeping children safe. A classroom where education should take place is not where any adult should primarily focus on being well-liked. Instead, the focus of the teacher needs to be on maintaining a classroom where students can learn. The teacher needs to work at being a well-respected disciplinarian who has to be assertively tough when necessary. The teacher needs to let students find their own friends who are their own age. A teacher, who isn't in the profession to be part of the academic team that disciplines children as needed, ends up undermining what the conscientious disciplinarians and teachers are trying to accomplish. Teachers whose primary goal is to be popular are selfish by taking away from the efforts of the good teachers as well as taking away some of the groundwork the students need in their formative years. Fortunately, some teachers, who are overly-engaged in trying to be nothing more than popular with the students, do not last. Yet, I have seen some of them survive somehow, and they unfortunately continue their detrimental ways.

The worst such case that I witnessed like this was when I had to work with a woman who went beyond wanting to be her students' best friend. Unfortunately, I was stuck on a team of teachers with her for at least one school year, as I recall. The last year I had to work on a team with her was the very worst. When her students went to any other teacher's classroom besides hers, her students turned into a roomful of extremely resentful children. The students acted as though they wanted nothing to do with other teachers who had the responsibility of teaching them at different times throughout the day. The other teachers, including me, had an incredibly bad time with this group. The students' main classroom teacher, who obviously wanted to be the students' best friend, turned the students against any teacher that made them sit, behave, and do school work. That teacher not only wanted to be every student's best friend, but she obviously worked consciously at getting the students to dislike having to go to anyone else's classroom. When the students were made to behave or do work in other classrooms, they would often threaten to tell their primary teacher as if she would see to it that other teachers would be punished for not letting them do as they pleased. Their primary teacher openly criticized other teachers in front of the students and sided with them most every time there was a concern involving a student's academics, grades, and discipline. More than the classroom of students, the teacher was a nightmare! She, and not the students, created the worst teaching experience I had in all the years that I taught.

The next year, I had that same group of students in one of my classes again for yet another 45-minute class every school day. They were now assigned to another primary teacher. The horrendous primary teacher now had a new group of students and had nothing to do with her last year's group of students. The class-from-hell, as teachers sometimes referred to the group, didn't have any teachers like the woman who apparently insisted on being their best friend the previous year. Fortunately, the students were assigned to a primary teacher who was like the rest of the students' team of teachers, in that she was conscientious, professional, and a strong disciplinarian. Being assigned to such a team of teachers for their last year at the school was what this group needed, and the school's principal must have realized it after the disastrous year many teachers and the students had had the previous year. The second year I taught the group, that former incredibly bad class became my best class in terms of behavior and effort to learn. I was amazed at the change, which I credited to those students being away from the previous year's teacher and then being assigned to a very good primary teacher.

Near the end of that school year, I spoke with the principal about the experiences of having lived through an incredibly hellacious year and then a great year with the same group of students. I explained how it was apparent to me that having a different main classroom teacher made the difference. The second time around with the group of students, they had an older woman who was respectfully firm, fair, and consistent in her dealings with the students. She had apparently been around long enough to have an admirable reputation among teachers for taking no nonsense from anyone, including the students, other teachers, and her superiors. There was a need in me to let my boss know, in case she hadn't figured it out already, that most of the problems that the group of students had the previous year were not the fault of the students. The fault needed to be handed to their last year's primary teacher. The group of students truly turned out to be a great class who could learn and behave properly after all. I could only assume that my boss went to the students' previous primary teacher and had a serious talk with her, because that teacher stared daggers at me from then until the day I retired, approximately two years. In spite of the stared daggers, I can only hope that the information I gave to the boss finally straightened the ineffective teacher out. That teacher needed to be addressed by someone in a supervisory position for the benefit of any students and staff members who ever had to work with her since those horrendous experiences many teachers had with her on a teaching team.

Again, when it comes to teaching children, I've done it for decades. Teach the children well. Discipline the children just as well. It doesn't mean you can't conduct yourself in a way that will make you liked by them or popular with them. There were classrooms in which I was quite well-liked and popular. There were other classrooms in which I wasn't so well-liked because I had to exert my disciplinary skills to maintain a learning environment for all of my students in some classes. Each class is different, of course, depending on the mixture of students in each class. Regardless of popularity or lack of it, when I see former students out and about, I am gratified to find that they have respect for me in their future years. Their show of respect is extremely gratifying. For that displayed respect, I am very grateful to them.

Regardless of how popular an educator awkwardly needs to be with students, he or she must not sacrifice the children's needs. The students need to be taught and disciplined for their best future. Many of the students will realize it and appreciate it in time. If adults have a need to be popular, maybe they could run for political office with their alleged charm. They definitely should not, however, disrupt a child's learning process by becoming teachers who appear to be in the profession to satisfy their personal insecurity problem of needing to be liked by kids. Again, I've seen it happen and it does not result in teaching the children well. It doesn't help the other educators, either, who are trying to do honorably right by the students of which they have been assigned to educate.

Finally, in spite of my strong assertions that youngsters need to be properly educated and disciplined for the best possible lives ahead of them, adults need to remember that they are children. Every child deserves his or her one childhood. Being a child should give one the right to make mistakes from which he or she can learn. Therefore, beyond the consequences for a child's errors being firm, fair, and consistent, the consequences should be given with compassionate understanding.

Chapter Twenty-Four

Diversify your jobs

Change jobs throughout life, if possible. If changing jobs isn't logical, take on second jobs that give you a wider perspective on life and on people. As a teacher, I had a great opportunity to diversify my second jobs. After all, with eight weeks or more off during the summer, there was no reason I couldn't try other jobs during my time away from the classroom. Yes, eight weeks is about all I got off with required training and preparation for the following school year. Those who think all teachers get three months off are wrong. If there is any teacher that truly got a full three months off during the summer when I was a full-time teacher, I never met the person.

Besides, back in the day, working during the summer was often a necessity for a teacher, who was the sole wage-earner in a household, rather than an option. The reason was that teaching paid very little money for a time. I, for example, started teaching full-time in 1972 for $7,200 a year. That scarcely covered my bills, including rent and car expenses, for the months I taught. Therefore, I needed to make money during the summer months because the bills obviously didn't stop coming in when the school year ended in June. Where I first taught, I was warned that most teachers at the school where I was teaching had husbands who made money to pay their families' bills. I was not-so-humorously told, "The teachers' salaries are just the husband's beer money around here."

Fortunately, it was never difficult for me to find a job at the beginning of the summer as I worked somewhere every summer during my early teaching years. Also, I not only had a summer job every summer, back in the day, but I also had a second job during the school year. At one point, I had two part-time jobs while teaching. For self-satisfaction, I always applied for part-time jobs that I had often wanted to try. I went after jobs I thought I'd not only enjoy but would even learn something from doing. My thought was that there was no job too small or too insignificant for me to do. The attitude that I was doing a job for the enjoyment and experience of it, as well as for the money, helped me through the extremely busy times in my life.

Those part-time jobs included being a disco DJ at a couple of night clubs, working for a brief period at three very different radio stations in the Chicagoland area in which one played polkas and easy listening music while the other two aired pop music with a good amount of local news and weather, clerking at a Musicland record store, doing counter and register chores at a Dunkin Donuts, being the night manager at a restaurant which included all positions during the six-week training period for the job, writing web pages at a downtown Chicago bank using HTML back in the day, doing delivery jobs as a courier for a couple of Chicago area delivery companies, and more. Having done a variety of part-time jobs on top of teaching has made my life much more interesting than it would have been. In my retirement years, if I come across a job that I've always wanted to do, I'll probably apply for it. Doing other jobs gives one an understanding and even an appreciation for what others do in a wide variety of employment fields. It's good for a person to have as many experiences in life as possible, including job experiences. Of course, beyond a second job, one can get a sense of what others do in life by volunteering at different organizations, such as a library, a church, a shelter, a food pantry, a senior center, and so many more places.

## Chapter Twenty-Five

Respect people

My number one lesson that children need to be taught included the advice that everyone needs to respect people. Be respectful and respect will most likely be returned to you. Beyond respecting people to their face, respect them when they aren't around. It is best not to talk negatively about anyone, including time you might be talking behind a person's back. Your negative talk about someone may make you look even worse than the person of whom you are negatively speaking. To make it worse, the person you have spoken against may hear what you've said about him or her in the past. Then, to make the bad situation even worse, the person who repeats what you've said against someone may do so inaccurately by telling an incredibly worse account of what you actually said. Unfortunately, I speak from personal experience here.

A janitor at the school where I taught took a break from cleaning my room after school some days and talked to me as I prepared for the next school day. One late afternoon, he started bad-mouthing another janitor who was on medical leave from our school. The janitor who spoke to me claimed that the other janitor was abusing the school district by claiming that she had some sort of medical condition that was caused on the job. He said she was constantly taking off work with pay for extended periods of time when it wasn't necessary. He said that she was feeling well enough to work but was just lazy and abusing the system. In time, she returned to work but was put at a desk in the school's office rather than given her janitorial duties due to her alleged medical concern.

Sometime later, I was talking with a couple of teachers after school while this gossipy janitor was cleaning the room. I repeated what he had said about the other janitor abusing the system. I concluded my comments by saying that secretary's day was coming up, and even though I had always bought something for every person who works in the school's office, I wouldn't be buying anything for the janitor-turned-clerk because she really wasn't a secretary. Additionally, she was still getting paid quite well as a janitor and was making more money than she would have if she was getting paid as an office clerk.

In time, the janitor-turned-clerk made my life hell by continually going out of her way to work against me. On some occasions, a parent or one of my family members called the school and told her on the office phone that I should return a call. Other than emergencies, teachers were not to be interrupted during their classes at our school. Unfortunately, I never got the messages that people had left for me. Consequently, parents of my students and some of my family members were extremely irritated with me because I wasn't returning calls. After these unfortunate instances occurred a number of times within a month or so, I confronted the woman and asked her why she wasn't giving me my messages. She turned away, angrily mumbled something under her breath, and refused to even speak directly to me.

The problems with her unprofessional conduct even got worse with me not being given necessary information to perform my job to the best of my ability as a teacher at the school. Eventually, the only solution I could think of was to go to one of my superiors and tell her what was going on with this woman. The boss, the janitor-turned-office clerk, and I had a meeting in the principal's office. The janitor-turned-office clerk said, basically, that she was upset because I had said negative things about her. Having totally forgotten that I had repeated to a couple of fellow-teachers what the other janitor had told me about her abusing medical leave, I adamantly denied that I had talked negatively about her. In front of the boss, I told the janitor-turned-clerk, "If you don't like me, you can spit at me when you see me at the mall! But I work hard at being a professional at my job here, and I'm not going to let you or anyone else continue ruining my reputation by not communicating with me and giving me my messages." At that, the boss called the head secretary into the office and told her that my situation was yet another problem she was having with this woman in the office. She told the head secretary to give the woman different duties that did not include answering the phones. As I recall, the woman ended up in the copy room to either run off papers or sit there with nothing to do.

Then, I remembered. I finally remembered that I did repeat what the other janitor had told me. At first, I didn't want to believe that he would be so low as to get me in trouble with the woman by telling her that I had said what he had actually told me. After an investigation, it was obvious that the janitor who had bad-mouthed her to me in the first place had turned around and told her that I had talked against her. He may have even spiced the story up by saying that I wasn't going to buy her a gift for secretary's day when I was gifting the other ladies in the office. Of course, the gossiping janitor never would have told the janitor-turned-clerk that I got all of my negative information about her from him. By the time I had figured it out, the janitor-turned-office clerk had been moved to another school's office in the school district as, from what I understood, other teachers and other office personnel at our school found her to be very difficult.

What I learned from that extremely unfortunate incident was to never talk behind someone's back. In this instance, I felt very bad about it because, prior to all of this, I really liked talking to both janitors after school. I had considered them to be work-related friends before the unfortunate episodes. Following these unfortunate episodes, other than exchanging a brief greeting, I avoided talking to the gossipy janitor. In time, there were rumors about him, and he was gone from our school, too. From that episode until the day I retired from that school, I continued to hear all kinds of gossip about all kinds of people. Though I was an avid listener, I refused to add as much as a word.

I painfully remember the incident with the two janitors at school all too well. The incident reminds me never to gossip. Again, gossip not only may get back to the person that is being gossiped about, but it may be manipulated in a way that makes things uncomfortable and extremely bad for the person doing the gossiping. Beyond not gossiping, show respect for people. Respect people, even when stories about them are unattractive and even when they aren't around.

Chapter Twenty-Six

Keep it light-hearted

One ought to keep things humorous when occasions and opportunities permit one to do so. One of the best feelings in life is having a hearty laugh. To some of us, it is just as great a feeling to make another person laugh. A laugh and a smile can improve one's day immensely. One doesn't have to be a trained or natural-born comedian to say something light-hearted. While one doesn't need to try to be a comedian 24 hours a day, obviously, lifting another person's spirits with humor and a smile in proper proportion is a very good personality trait.

Besides friends and acquaintances, one can generously humor people they meet when they are out and about. Myself, I enjoy trying to liven up service people's days. I believe it's more than appropriate to humor people who are doing a job for me and other people. After all, waiting on people isn't always an easy job and many times the financial rewards aren't very good either. With the many part-time jobs I've had through the years, I've been there and done that. Besides livening up people's day somewhat, they may give a response that will give you a smile and a chuckle as well. Whether it's a waiter, a cashier, a drive-thru employee at a food establishment or a bank, a barber, the person who answers the call when calling a business or radio station's talk show or contest line, a dentist, a doctor, a car mechanic, or a library employee, giving them a reason to smile is possible.

For example, next time a server or drive-thru employee at a restaurant asks you how you're doing, robustly tell him you're hungry and see the smile that you've created. I've told regular servers at restaurants I often patronize, "I'm hungry every time I see you!" Almost guaranteed to get a laugh is when a service person asks how I am and I say, "Fine... but I lie a lot." You don't have to be one of those customers who always insincerely says 'fine' or just ignores the question and says, 'I'll start out with a cup of coffee.' Of course, when the check comes at the end of a meal, you could look at the bill quickly, hold it to your chest, look the server in the eye, and then lower your voice and ask, 'Where's the back door?' When I pay cash and the cashier struggles with dollar bills, I say, "It's okay if they stick together." Most cashiers get a kick out of that one while others don't get it. One crabby cashier started lecturing me on how much trouble she would be in if the bills stuck together and I got too much change back. Rather than explaining the obvious, which is that I was only joking, I just took my correct change and left. You can't charm or humor them all.

Don't stifle yourself from the spontaneity of being humorous. Calling a radio station over and over again that was going to gift the 100th caller with a pair of tickets to a concert, my call was finally answered and I excitedly said, "Caller number 100 here!" The person answering the phone paused and said, "Yes, you are!" Then there were the times I have been stopped by policemen on the street. I found that a little humor might help. One night, I was returning along a lonely street from my late-evening English class in the Chicago suburbs. I moved from the right lane to the left lane in preparation of a left turn far down the street. Out of nowhere, so it appeared, a police car was behind me with its lights lighting up the night. When the officer approached me, he asked, "Do you know why I stopped you?" I said that I had no clue. He said, "You moved over a lane without signaling." I seriously asked, "Who was I supposed to be signaling to? Nobody was on the street but me." He smiled, agreed that I'd made a good point, but still wrote me a warning. I said, "I'm just curious. Why are you writing it up if it's just a warning and I don't have to pay a fine?" He said that they have to document every stop they make. I asked, "It helps your racial profiling data by stopping a white guy, too, right?" He laughed uncomfortably, finished writing the warning, and we parted ways.

Back in the day, when I bought lottery tickets, I used to tell the clerk to blow on the ticket for good luck. Though they usually laughed and just gave me the ticket. Other times, some female clerks would actually blow on the ticket and laugh as they gave it to me. The most memorable time was when an older man, quite possibly the owner of the gas station I was at, was working the lottery machine. I hesitated before using my comment because he didn't look like he'd be easy to humor, but I went for it anyway. As he grabbed the ticket coming out of the machine, I said, "Blow on it for good luck!" He thrust the ticket at my chest and said, "I'm not blowing on anything!" Then he pointed at the door as if to tell me to get out of there while the younger guys working behind the counter laughed uncontrollably.

Naturally, the service person may sometimes humor you as well. A dentist said that a procedure I needed to have performed would only take 45 minutes while also informing me that the cost would be $1,000. Honesty took control of me, and I surprised myself by blurting out, "$1,000 for 45 minutes?" Without skipping a beat, he said, "OK, I can make it last three hours."

It's not that I'm never serious with people who serve me, because I am. However, when opportunity knocks for displaying a light personality, I do it. I especially do it when the person's face reveals that his or her day could use an emotional lift. After all, I love when someone improves my day by giving me a reason to smile, and I want to do the same for others.

As far as some stranger giving me a hearty laugh, one recent incident was very awkward. I was relieving myself late one night on my way home when there was absolutely no place to stop and do so. No, I didn't have a bottle or a big cup in the car either. There was absolutely no place to use a restroom, or, I swear, I would have done so. The truth is, since I am on the road so often, I could probably write a book about washroom experiences that occur while I have been traveling, and I just might someday. Anyway, I was quite certain I had found a safe place to relieve myself at the end of a funeral home parking lot where there were a couple of cars parked. I assumed those cars belonged to people who lived in the apartment building just beyond the parking lot. Shocked, as I was urinating, I heard the sound of a car window being lowered. I looked and saw there was a man and a woman in one of the cars a short distance from where I was standing beside my car. The woman said, "Can I hold it?" I lied and embarrassingly said, "Oh, I'm sorry. I'm working and couldn't find a washroom." She said, "Working? So am I." The man in the car with her cringed. That gave me a good chuckle all the way home.

Be prepared to run into some people who apparently want you to be as miserable as they are when you're displaying a sense of humor. Case in point, I had a student who tried to squelch my good mood and humor by responding to my comedic effort by saying, "You're trying to be funny, aren't you?" To that, I said, "What do you mean by saying that I'm trying to be funny? I'm a riot!" When I was a child, one of my best friends, now I wonder why, continually let me know that my attempt at humor was unappreciated. It didn't stop me from trying to be appreciated with it, though. As an adult, I have seen him a couple of times, and he hasn't changed. Fifty years later, he still has inappropriate sarcastic remarks when anyone around him tries to lighten the mood. I try not to let another person's personality problem become mine. Don't stifle others from attempting to be light-hearted or comedic, and don't let others stifle you. Keeping it light at appropriate times is good for a person, inside and out, as well as being good for a person's likeability and amicable reputation.

Chapter Twenty-Seven

Let people know what you want

Before complaining that you aren't getting what you want out of life professionally and beyond, do all you can for yourself by letting others know your needs and desires. While it may take courage to state your desires and goals to others, it may be necessary for you to get what you want out of life. As a young teacher, I would sometimes feel bad when another teacher would be asked to join committees or to do some tasks I wasn't asked to do. I'd think, 'Why him instead of me? Doesn't the boss think I could do that?' In time, I realized that my superiors may have chosen others because the others were more vocal than I was about wanting a leadership role in the school. I was quite correct. As soon as I started volunteering myself for different tasks and the boss knew I wanted to advance in my work, I became a go-to person when there was a position to be filled on a committee or when there were some other jobs to be performed. I really wanted to be on the inside track of making decisions for the schools I worked at rather than simply one of the persons who had to live and work via others' decisions. I learned to not just sit around and feel bad about not being chosen for various responsibilities, but to let the powers-that-be know I was very willing and completely capable of handling more responsibilities. After showing that I was wanting leadership roles, I went from being just another teacher to one who spent time as the PTA president, the academic team leader, one of the members of the school's leadership team, running an after-school technology program, working on promotional press releases for the school, running the school's newspaper, and administering the school's spelling bee leading up to district and county competitions. I was even our school's union representative for a time. While these responsibilities equated to much more work for me, they were worthwhile experiences that made me a more involved faculty member and a more experienced professional. Let people know what you want before thinking your extra efforts aren't wanted or needed.

Chapter Twenty-Eight

Reject racism

Racism, which comes in many different forms, is ugly. Racism matters in life, in society, and on the job. The first incident that struck me regarding race in my life was when I applied for a teaching job in a school district that was much different than the one where I had been teaching previously. I'm white, and I nearly didn't get a job that lasted nearly three decades because of my race. The man who ultimately hired me openly stated at the end of a successful interview for the English teaching job, "Everything sounds good! I want to hire you!" Then he lowered his voice and admitted, "But if a qualified black female walks in before the end of the week, she gets the job because I need minorities." Then he held up two fingers and explained, "By hiring a black female, I get two credits. One because she's black and one because she's a woman. I need minorities." Very fortunate for me, by the end of the week, no qualified minorities had apparently applied. Therefore, I got the job. This was the most dramatic way I learned at a young professional age that one's race certainly matters.

A few years after that incident, I was with a black friend at a restaurant-bar in a Chicago suburb on a cloudy June afternoon. That is when I disappointingly and shockingly learned about social rather than professional racism. My friend and I walked in the place and I saw a pool table in a side room off the restaurant's dining room. We decided to play a game before dining. As we were digging in our pockets to find quarters to put in the pool table and selecting cue sticks, a man from the restaurant stood in the doorway to the pool room and sternly announced, "We're closed!" Totally confused, I asked, "What?" The man said louder and more sternly, "We're closed! You'll have to leave!" I looked out at the people dining in the restaurant and assumed he meant we couldn't play pool. I soon realized, however, that the man wanted the two of us to leave the place entirely. My friend softly said, "Let's go. I know what's going on." I was slow to realize what was happening because I was totally foreign to anything like this. By the time we got out of the restaurant and back to the car, I realized that I had just witnessed social racism for the first time. Until that incident, I never gave any thought to my friend's skin color. I never imagined anyone would have a concern about my friend being black. To this day, the incident angers me more than words can express.

As years passed, I saw other forms of racism. I was riding through the South Side of Chicago on a warm summer's night with my car windows down. At a red light, a car with at least four adults and one child, all black people, stopped alongside of my car. The child, maybe seven years of age, started yelling obscenities and racist remarks at me. He repeatedly shouted, "You white motherfucker." As I refused to respond, he yelled, "Yeah, you hear me, you white motherfucker." I continued to ignore him. Incredibly, the adults with him in the car didn't stop him as the verbal abuse continued until the light turned green and I could take off. How incredibly ugly racism is. How young it can start in one's life. Furthermore, how disgusting the people are who apparently teach racism to children. I don't hate very much in life, but I admit to hating racism with a passion.

So as a U.S.-born white man who has been politically labeled in current times as a person who enjoys white privilege by society and the media, my point is that we are all negatively affected by racism. Admittedly, some are more impacted than others.

## Chapter Twenty-Nine

Value true friendships

True friends in your life may be few. Choose your circle of friends wisely while remembering that to have a true friend, one needs to be a true friend. Have friends who bring you up rather than down, and do the same uplifting for them. To continue receiving the benefits of a friendship, one needs to keep giving to that friend. If you aren't living up to the expectations of being a true friend, your unique friendships probably will not last. Fortunately, throughout my life, I have had some very good friends who totally understand that to have a friend, one needs to be a friend. They understand, as I have tried to practice, that the best gift you can give a friend is your time even when it may be difficult to find time to give. I've also found that when I see myself in someone else, he or she is a prime candidate for becoming a true friend. It has been said that you are a true friend to someone when you care for that person like a mother, you discipline the person like a father, you tease the person like a sister, and you make that friend miserable like a brother.

I've been disappointed in myself at times for having miscalculated some friendships by not having invested enough time into them. Contrarily, at other times, I may have invested too much time in a futile relationship that wasn't turning into a true friendship after all. Work at realizing who your real friends are and invest yourself primarily in those people. When you have found one of those rare people that you can truly count on, put them high on the list of people who can count on you, also. Decipher between people who are your true friends who care about you and your social-only friends who are simply good for hanging out together. While these social-only friends can be good for fun times, it's your true friends who you can always depend on that are special. More than that, they are spectacular.

Like many other people, I'm sure, I have mistaken social-only friends for being true friends. After much time in the friendship, it became apparent that they were just looking for fun times and, much too often, looking for help with their own needs. Though they were quick to repeatedly call on me in their times of need, they were repeatedly not available when I arrived at my time of needing help from them.

Unfortunately, there are people who never seem to realize or simply do not care that being a true friend has to be a two-way relationship for that type of friendship to continue. It's people who continually refuse to reciprocate true friendship who cause resentment, hurt feelings, and even anger. Of course, one should never do favors for another person with the expectation that they will get a one-on-one return for their good deeds. However, there is nothing wrong with expecting reciprocation of good deeds when one's own time of need arises.

Case in point, I had a friend who had no qualms about asking me to help him move into a new residence, calling on me repeatedly to give him rides to and from places, summoning my time and effort when needing references to get jobs, verbally giving advice the many times he thought others had slighted him, and so much more. I never imagined that he wouldn't jump at the chance to help me one day, too. The possibility that he wouldn't return a favor never crossed my mind.

Though I'm not one to burden anyone unless I have practically nowhere else to turn, my time finally came. One Sunday night, I had a car accident and desperately needed a ride to my home from the auto body shop where my car was towed. I called this friend because, of all the people I knew, he lived closest to the body shop where I was stranded and, so I felt, wouldn't mind helping me out. As soon as I got him on the phone and explained the situation, he asked, "Can't you call your sister?" I was shocked. While I don't remember exactly how I got home that night, as it happened a long time ago, I know it was without any help from him. Likely, I ended up calling a taxi for a very long and expensive ride home. Additionally, I wanted help in moving things from my wrecked car to the vehicle that would take me to my residence and then into my place. This so-called friend refused to help.

After that, I begrudgingly continued to help him when he asked me to help him out. Honestly, however, I didn't feel good about investing time or effort in helping him anymore. After a good number of years, the disappointment, sense of feeling that I was being used, and even anger over that situation in which he refused to assist me, built up to the point that I finally mentioned it one day. First, he denied it happened. When I was adamant in saying that it most certainly did happen, he accused me of leaving some details out of the story and claimed that he never would have done such a thing to me. The argument got to the point where I said, "I can't think of one time you've ever helped me when I've needed help in all the years I've known you." There was silence, as I'm sure he couldn't think of a time either. After a lengthy pause, he belittled me for bringing it up. I quit ever asking him for anything. He is a classic example of a social-only friend. I know I can't count on him for anything when I have my times of need. When I need assistance, I don't even think of asking him anymore.

As I wrote the first edition of this essay on true friendships, he asked me for assistance again. I suggested he ask another friend. He said that the other friend isn't dependable. Since I could make time to help him again, I came through for him again. However, I didn't do it willingly at all. It has been said that if you are not going to do something pleasantly, don't do it. Well, I helped him anyway. Though I don't feel very good about breaking my promise to myself to not assist him anymore, I know I would feel worse about myself if I didn't. Go figure.

Logically, as the years progress, needing assistance from others increases. Therefore, I find myself assisting older friends and acquaintances with the understanding that they really need help when they reach out for needed assistance. It feel it is the right thing to do while I am still at a point in life when I can help others. Though I am getting older, too, obviously, I still resist from asking anyone for assistance of any kind. Not only do I not like to bother anyone, but I fear the rejection of not getting the person's help. Other than a couple of times when I needed a ride a distance from home, I haven't asked anyone for anything. Thank God, my brother has come through the times I needed a ride.

Unfortunately, practically every time I have requested help in non-emergency situations from people, I have been refused or ignored. Fortunately, those non-emergency situations are things that I can do without or can pay to have done. It hurts, though, to see on Facebook that so-and-so spent a whole weekend helping someone move to a new house, while my request for an afternoon's assistance at my place is totally ignored or denied. In one instance, I was talking to someone about needing something done at my place, and the person said, "Ask 'so-and-so.' He did it for us!" The person was shocked when I said, "I already asked him, and he won't. Even though I offered to pay him to do it." Maybe it's something about me. Maybe it's something about these people who simply won't go out of their way when I need assistance. Regardless of what it is, it hurts.

Anyway, I have learned to not confuse social-only friends with true friends. Beware of those social friends who always have a problem and need assistance but are never available when your time of need arrives because the bitterness against them can mount. Realize they are good for fun times and leave it there. Depending on the circumstances in knowing someone, a social friendship or acquaintanceship can last many years. I have a good number of those.

Additionally, I have found that any family member or friend who continually disrespects me usually won't change his or her ways, regardless of the number of times I have let the person know that I feel mistreated by him or her. The longer I have put up with a disrespectful person in my life, the more validation the person thinks he or she has for continually engaging in the poor treatment of me.

The lesson is that the sooner you realize that you are trapped in a one-sided friendship that is all about the other person instead of being a respectful give-and-take friendship, the better. The sooner you get away from someone who continually disrespects you, the better. After all, being without a person doesn't have to mean lonely. In some situations, being without a particular person can be best.

As one very good friend once told me when I was burdened with a disrespectful person in my circle, "Sometimes a person has to divorce a friend." If a friend or family member is continually disrespectful, their disrespect may be attributed to a jealousy they have of you, or it may be for some reason that you will never understand. Actually, you really don't need to invest time and effort in trying to understand it. The bottom line is that if a person is not contributing anything positive to your life in spite of how hard you have tried to prove yourself as a good friend to him or her, divorce the person. Finding and keeping friends are like acquiring anything else of value in life. Sometimes it works out and sometimes it just wasn't meant to be.

Obviously, divorcing a friend due to disrespect is easier said than done because sometimes it is difficult to distance yourself from someone you have become accustomed to having in your life. You may try to reason that they have had some positivity on your life by occupying your free time. However, the benefit of distancing yourself from a disrespectful person, which will ease the built-up resentment, will outweigh any advantage. It is far better to get anyone who is continually bringing you down out of your life. It is very possible that a person who treats you disrespectfully may treat practically everyone he or she knows the hurtful way you have been treated. You don't have to be one of the people who is mistreated by that person. You can move on and look for better friendships, and then appropriately invest your time and efforts in the new relationships you may find.

On a similar note, one needs to understand that no matter how hard a person tries, there are some people who simply cannot be pleased.

Therefore, I have learned that I shouldn't spend too much time and effort on a person who can't ever be pleased with me or those who are apparently never going to like me, no matter what I say or do. Case in point was one guy that, to this day, I have never connected with, and Lord knows I tried. Though I would never call him a friend of mine, I tried diligently to get along with him because we worked at the same place and continually ended up in the same social circles. To my dismay, he continually went out of his way to either belittle me or ignore me. He seemed to relish in doing so. When we spoke, the sparkling personality that he displayed with others was absent. One day, years after I'd given up on even trying to befriend him anymore, I bluntly asked him what his problem was with me. Without pause he snapped with disgust, "You're too serious all the time." I was shocked at his response. I told him that he must have never gotten to know me because, as I asserted, "I'm not all that serious!" It's the truth. I definitely know how to have a good time with anyone who is willing to have one. Of course, I also wondered why he thought that he had license to disrespect me just because he thought I was serious. Though I appreciated a response from him, it didn't make a whole lot of sense to me.

Now that I'm retired from that job, I don't run into him anymore, fortunately. In retrospect, I spent way too much time trying to get this person to treat me better. I was much too frustrated over the lack of progress in my efforts to befriend him. Fast forwarding to several years later, I believe I finally realized the problem he had with me. He disapproved of some of the people I had as friends on the job. They weren't like him, which was his problem with being prejudiced.

Again, an important lesson I've learned in life is to understand that I can't please everyone, and investing too much time and effort in trying to please someone who can't be pleased becomes a frustrating waste of time and energy. I can't control another person's idiosyncrasies and prejudices. Yet, I can divorce that person from my life. I now know to give up on such a futile relationship if one should reoccur in my life.

In summation, it is important to decipher between social-only friends and true friends who are reciprocally dependable friends. When you find a social friend who has something to offer you and you have something to offer in return, enjoy your time together. Realize that those friendships come and go. Primarily invest time and effort on your true friends. First and foremost, be there for them. Some friends turn out to be an open expressway in your life while others become a traffic jam. You are in total control of analyzing the map and choosing which routes to take.

This has been the most difficult essay or chapter I have written for this book because it is extremely difficult to swallow my pride and to admit that I have misread people of whom I believed I could count on. Perhaps, in time, having put the disappointments in writing may help me. Time will tell. If nothing else, if you are concerned about people having disappointed you, you now know that you are not alone.

Chapter Thirty

Decide if love is for you

I figure a book about life's lessons ought to include something about love or the lack of it. After all, love is one of our strongest emotions, whether it is a love of life, people, places, things, or simply ideas. As much as I may have liked skipping this topic all together, it would be a glaring omission if I didn't say something about it. My basic belief about love is that, when all else fails, one can take comfort in knowing that one can work at loving himself while remembering that he or she is always loved by God.

With that said, if you fall in love or think you have fallen in love but, deep down, you know it just isn't going to work out, give it time. Hopefully, you'll snap out of it. Then again, in time, you might be discarded by your partner who may have realized the relationship isn't working before you realize it. There is absolutely no reason good enough to rush into a relationship of which you or your partner has doubts. There is also absolutely no reason good enough to try to force a person to stay in a relationship that either person doubts. When it comes to making a commitment like marriage, it is no time for a person to test his or her ability to take risks. Be certain.

There were several times I thought I might have fallen in love. In time, I realized I was wrong. In due time, I found that the initial fascination started to wane too quickly. Of course, the initial fascination always wanes somewhat, doesn't it? Anyway, with me, I liked being with the person, enjoyed conversations, and going out. However, in time, I could not envision waking up next to the person every morning and going home to the person every night. Though I was careful not to utter the words 'I love you,' some people, who the two of us knew, were asking when I was going to get engaged. Though the notion that I would get engaged never came from me, I was sometimes considered the bad guy for never proposing marriage. In other words, I never saw myself as a heartbreaker, but maybe I was. Fortunately, I'm not a person who responds to peer pressure very often. Furthermore, I never respond to peer pressure when it is something as serious and life-changing as getting married.

The time when the fascination of being in love, for lack of a better term, begins to wane is a tough time because you really want the great feeling of being close to another person to last forever. You may think that the initial fascination is going to return when there is no logical reason that it will. If you feel a relationship isn't going to last, regardless of the reason, accept the wake-up call by giving it appropriate thought. Then reacting to it. Don't wait. Waiting for a relationship to mysteriously dissolve on its own may take too long.

Here's how it may happen. One person is desperately waiting for the alleged love part of the relationship to dissipate while the other is mentally planning a wedding. Of course, many people who know the two of them are thinking there will be a wedding, too. While you may wish that the two of you could just be friends forever and not let love ruin the friendship, I have never personally known that to turn out real well. It is probably best to let it go and to move on. Everyone is different, though. Some people I have known have remained friends after having lost that loving feeling.

When a relationship is headed south, odds are that the waning of fascination won't occur at the same time for both people if, in fact, it does occur for both of them. It's tough when one person needs condolences for the lost relationship and the other one ought to be congratulated for realizing the relationship just wasn't meant to be. If a relationship doesn't turn out to be everything one expected it to be, I believe that he or she should let the relationship end sooner than later. There is no reason to prolong the inevitable.

On a final note about love, it appears that there are people who can't live without a partner in their lives. I feel sorry for them. For them, I wrote a song in the 1980s called "Being Alone Doesn't Mean Lonely." I'll never understand why Reba McEntire wouldn't record it. Then again, it's not too late, Reba! Also, there are people who can't live with a partner in their lives. For them, I also feel sorry. For them, I wrote many songs. For some people, and this is the most important sentence in this essay about love, love takes a great deal of work that some people aren't willing to or able to give. People who aren't willing or able to totally invest themselves in a love relationship should not disrupt the potential love life of another person who wants and is capable of having a love relationship. It is selfishly wrong to lead someone on.

Chapter Thirty-One

Stay out of debt

Don't get so far in financial debt that it runs, or should I say ruins, your life for a time. At some point I had to quit spending more money than I was earning or, I truly believe, I would have reached a point where I may have possibly never gotten out of debt. That's a gross exaggeration, but you get the idea. With me, the realization that I had to quit spending so much money finally sunk in sometime around my 30$^{th}$ year on the planet when the credit card bills were coming at me with a vengeance. Though I was always a very good math student, I basically refused to apply my math skills to my own finances simply because I loved going out and spending money. I worked very hard. Therefore, I so much wanted to believe that working hard justified playing hard. Sadly, how hard I worked had little to do with having enough money to pay my bills for a time. I needed to bring in more money than I was spending, and I wasn't doing it. I needed to grow up, financially, and be responsible to myself and my lenders. I got to the point when I realized that my proverbial tomorrow may financially never come. I needed to start bringing in more money than I was spending every month. Another way of looking at it is to finally have admitted that I needed to spend less money than I was making every month. Fortunately, the lesson was eventually learned.

Back in the day, adding all of the minimum credit card bills that were due each month could scarcely be paid on my earnings. Though I was working a full-time job as well as a part-time job, I had to put most of the money I made on my credit card bills. It was hell. I had a limited amount of money to live on, and party on, after paying the bills. Something had to change. Of course, getting a part-time job was a good first step to get out of debt. The hours spent working a full-time and a part-time job equated to less time for going out and spending money. Life wasn't as much fun, but it was apparent to me that working practically all the time was what I had to do to change my dismal financial situation. By the age of 30, I had ignored the problem long enough. Maybe it was turning 30 and finally feeling older that made me take action. I was teaching full-time, doing all the extra duties I could get my hands on for extra cash at school, which included doing the much-dreaded lunch duty every day as well as other laborious duties. On top of that, for a time, I was also working two part-time jobs instead of just one. It took several years of that grueling schedule to get out of credit card debt. Remembering that unpleasant period in my life has helped me not repeat my financial mistakes.

I didn't turn things around by continually paying off the credit cards with high interest. First, I borrowed money from someone I knew and paid off all the credit cards. Quite incredibly, I eventually figured out that the person was charging me as much interest as a bank would charge me. Thinking back on it, I probably went to him first because I thought a loan officer at a bank would laugh me out of the bank. Though I was flattered a person I knew trusted me enough to give me the huge loan, there was absolutely no financial benefit for paying this person off instead of a bank. For one thing, paying a bank off on time boosted my credit rating.

Another issue with borrowing money from an individual rather than a bank was that, shocking to me, my personal lender was telling people that I had needed to borrow money from him while paying him back with interest. How embarrassing! After that personal humiliation, I swallowed my nerve and went to a bank. I was delighted to find out that I could get a loan at a decent rate. In fact, it was a slightly better rate than I had agreed to with the acquaintance. The bank classified the loan as a home improvement loan, if memory serves me right. After that visit to the bank, I immediately paid off my acquaintance in full, as part of the agreement we had had allowed me to pay the loan off early without penalty. I have never borrowed a penny from anyone since.

Ultimately, I paid one doable bill, my bank loan bill, every month instead of a pile of minimum payments to credit card companies every month. I recommend this to anyone who needs to get out of debt. Quit trying to pay off huge credit card debt by making monthly payments to credit card companies. I also advise skipping the assistance of an acquaintance who wants to supposedly help with a loan that includes interest. Besides, like in my situation, the person may tell your personal business to others, which is something I assume most people do not want broadcast. Instead, go to a bank. If, and only if, the bank won't help you because your finances are that bad, then maybe you'll want to find a real good acquaintance who has your best interest at heart and won't overly charge you with interest. Unfortunately, another suggestion is bankruptcy. I don't know much about it because, fortunately, I never filed for it. If one is in debt, he or she should be serious about getting out of debt. Do it now. It will only get worse if you don't. Money isn't everything, but I've found that being able to pay bills on time gives comfort.

Chapter Thirty-Two

Balance time for self, others, and work

When I turned 30, it was funny to see people treated me sympathetically due to the humorous notion that one has reached old age when he or she hits 30. Turning 30 didn't bother me at all. However, I did start feeling like my years were passing too quickly when I turned 31. I was feeling down on my 31st birthday. This birthday wasn't a joke. I felt like I really was too old too fast. Now, of course, I would love to be 31 again. When I turned 31, I had only been in teaching for about a decade and I was starting to feel somewhat bogged down by the responsibilities of having to work so hard. I really wasn't enjoying myself on the job as much as I was when it was new to me. One thing I always liked about teaching was that every day was a new challenge and quite different from most previous days. Though that kept things interesting much of the time, the routine of rushing out the door in the morning to get to school by 7:30 and being imprisoned in that classroom until 5:00 or later many Mondays through Fridays was beginning to take its toll on my life. I'm the type of teacher who couldn't leave the building until I had everything ready for the next day. If I wasn't totally prepared with materials laid out including handouts at my fingertips on my desk, tomorrow's date and an outline of tomorrow's activities written across the chalkboard with the note to the janitor that boldly stated "SAVE" so that he wouldn't erase the board, and more, I couldn't relax at night. I had to be ready to go when I walked in the classroom the next day. Even then, however, I would go home and somehow find more schoolwork to do or think about. That was my life from Monday through Friday for years. Yes, I was a prime case of anyone who is over-conscientious about his work and one who worries too much about his work. Consequently, I lived for the weekend.

On the weekend, if I wasn't working a part-time job all weekend, I would practically party myself beyond repair by going out with or without friends and family. In time, my weekends felt as though they were unrealistically getting out of control. There were Mondays when I felt that I was getting some badly needed rest by going back to work. Something had to change because it was not comfortable for me. All work for five days and all carefree living for two days, week after week, didn't seem right. It didn't appear to be sustainable. So, I made a change to balance my days, and in the process, balanced my life to be more livable. Even though I still spent what was undoubtedly too many hours at school so I wouldn't have to worry about the next school day when I left the building, I started getting my mind off of my job as much as I could in the evening by doing other things during the week. By balancing other things into my day that didn't involve work, I ended up going to bed more relaxed with other things besides my job on my mind. Besides improving my weekdays, it helped my weekends settle down somewhat as well. I was no longer feeling like I had to cram all the socially-good times into two days because I was actually allowing a small amount of time for relaxation and good times away from school during the weekday evenings when I didn't have to clock into a part-time job, too.

I highly recommend that everyone, especially workaholics like I was, balance their time spent working with time for self and for others on a nearly daily basis. By making time for other activities besides work, it helps one from resenting work. Now that I'm retired from teaching full-time, I find balancing is still important. Balancing some chores or work into my schedule is necessary because too much free time, believe it or not, isn't much better than spending too much time working. During retirement, balancing newly-discovered self-time and time for others with work-time can prevent boredom and keep one's mind and body active. A balanced life is a good life.

This is a good time to add that people ought to be good to themselves. They need to make an effort to keep themselves well. After all, when people don't keep themselves well, they aren't as well as they could be, otherwise, to themselves and others. A balanced life can assist one in being mentally, physically, and medically healthy.

Chapter Thirty-Three

Don't be overly satisfied

While being satisfied with accomplishments when warranted, never be overly satisfied to the extent that you don't work at improving yourself. Make the results of your life's work the best it can be. In my work, I have never quite reached the point of being so totally satisfied with myself that I allowed myself to stop trying harder to achieve more or to make a good situation even better. The best people among society seem to have had that attitude in their work, whether it has been people in business, education, sports, politics, or most any other type of work.

I think of the teachers I had, like one of my college English professors, who made me rewrite essays four times or more before putting the treasured grade of A on the paper. I think of the impact my parents had on me by acknowledging my successes but yet expecting even more from me. I think of the stories I've heard through the years about the musicians, writers, and movie-makers who were never totally satisfied with their products. With such an attitude, they turned out some of the best music, books, and movies the world has ever known.

Strive to do your best to accomplish more than you ever thought possible when you set out to do a task. On a personal level, I worked for a superior who was, in my opinion, the best school leader for whom I ever worked during my more than four decades of being in the teaching profession. She tempered the continual gratitude she expressed to her teachers in the trenches by asserting that we could always do better. She admitted that she could do better at what she was doing, too. Of course, she was correct on all counts. She led the school with the notion that regardless of how much we had accomplished in teaching the students, we could accomplish more. She took a very troubled-school from being a disciplinary and educational disaster, in my opinion, and turned it into a disciplined institution of learning where students developed a higher regard for education.

With her guidance, education took place at a pace that was not achieved before she was given the responsibility of running the school. Yet, as scores and discipline improved greatly under her leadership, she kept her teachers and students in check with respectful reminders that asserted we could even do better. With the support of the many of the staff members who bought into her strong beliefs, the school continued to improve.

I have always kept my eye on improving my work. It does not mean that I am not ever satisfied with myself because that wouldn't be good either. It means that I am aware that improving most anything is possible.

Then there is the question of how long a person should work. I believe a person should keep working at something as long as he or she is mentally and physically able. Keeping a mind and body vibrant is likely the key to longevity for many people. There should be no amount of good work and success in one's life that justifies him or her to stop working at something or to stop making contributions and accomplishments. Beyond what it does for the individual, it can do a great deal for others. Witnessing someone who works hard and achieves motives others, especially when the hard-working person is at a point in life when he or she doesn't necessarily have to work so diligently anymore. Strive to be all you can be, and when you think you have achieved it all, continue yearning to achieve more. Again, it does a mind and body a great amount of respectable good.

## Chapter Thirty-Four

## Read

Read endlessly. It will teach you a great deal. It will teach you many things about people, places, things, ideas, and life. It will also teach you to write so that you can express and share your thoughts and knowledge. Though I always enjoyed reading, I didn't always take the appropriate time to enjoy that pleasure in my life. I regret I hadn't taken time sooner to enjoy reading as I do now. Though I wasn't much of a novel reader until recent years, I have taken a limited amount of time to read materials on topics that interested me for as long as I can remember. I have always enjoyed reading about and learning about current events, politics, entertainment trends, and the academics of which I found interesting. In the old days, I skimmed daily newspapers. In more recent times, I go online to do some of my reading on a nearly daily basis.

I chose this time in my life to include this lesson because this is approximately the age when I finally began finding a little more time to enjoy reading. As previously mentioned, I began reading or listening to audio-books of fiction novels in recent times to witness the types of writings that publishers are publishing and that people are enjoying because one of my goals is to write well-received works. In the process, I have enjoyed reading others' stories more than I had ever thought I would. For me, reading a wide variety of materials is time spent enjoyably and well. Reading, I also believe, keeps my mind active. Additionally, reading extensively can keep a person more interesting for conversation and socializing with others because a reader is more informed and more aware than he or she would be otherwise. More singularly, reading occupies one's time with its informative as well as entertainment value. If you can get to a library or computer, it's a worthwhile activity that can be without any financial cost. As I write the updated version of "Life's Lessons," the rage is e-books, which are either free or very economically priced. Currently, I continually have at least one book in progress on my devices, which makes reading easy at most any location.

Chapter Thirty-Five

Write

I was going to combine reading and writing as one of life's most valuable lessons. However, I decided that writing has been just as important as reading in my life and should have an entry of its own. It should follow reading since reading helps one learn to write. When I started taking time to enjoy and benefit myself by reading more, I began spending more time writing. It was something that I had dabbled in for a long time prior to this time in my life, but I never took the craft of writing beyond my school work seriously until this point.

As a teacher, I challenged myself by writing articles about education. As a musician and fan of recorded and live music, I have written articles about music. I was encouraged greatly when I found my efforts were rewarded by getting published in various magazines. Then, I began getting serious about my need to be creative. Though I had written a few songs in my younger years, I got serious about creating songs, both words and melodies, at this time in my life. In time, I started promoting my songs to publishers. Some got published, and some of them even got recorded. I never had the big hit I had always wanted, but I found some contentment with the minimal success I found through the 1980s and early 1990s. I spent a lot of time working at the craft of songwriting and don't regret it. Socially, my life improved, too, as I went to songwriting seminars offered in the Chicago area and met people with like-interests. Some of those songwriters co-wrote songs with me for years, and we are still friends to this day.

During these years, if I wasn't busy with my jobs, I was sometimes reading and more often writing. It was a good time in my life. Beyond creative songwriting being an outlet for my creativity, I eventually found that reading something, and then writing about my reactions to what I had read, to be satisfying. Having read a great deal about politics, I have formed my own opinions and have written about those opinions. I got satisfaction in seeing those writings shared online via a website that posted my articles. Those writings even gave me a small amount of money when the articles would get enough readings or online clicks by readers. The now defunct website was called Examiner. Some of my political articles ended up on a CBS website, which paid me as well.

Even if one doesn't find a profit in writing, however, it is a worthwhile activity just like reading can be. Both reading and writing can be beneficial for one's mind. Additionally, the activities can occupy a great deal of one's time without expense. One can write to entertain others or to share his or her own knowledge and thoughts. Another personal advantage of writing is that it helps one sort out his or her thoughts. Sometimes I don't completely understand my own thoughts until I take time to go through the writing process with them. Taking time to think things out and then to put those thoughts in written form can be beneficial. This is apparent, I am sure, in that I'm writing a book such as this one.

The main reason I am writing this book is because any thoughts I have, like anyone else's thoughts, maximizes their meanings when they are shared. If one's thoughts are never shared, they die with him or her one day. As one can see, I am a person who wants my thoughts to have meaning, and therefore I share my thoughts on life. Naturally, some of my thoughts encompass other persons' thoughts that I have read and heard throughout my life. Hopefully, some of what a reader has gathered from my written thoughts will become part of his or her thoughts and beliefs in the future. And so it will go.

Beyond personal writings, writing documentations such as business letters is a skill worth developing. Back in the days of the typewriter, I wrote many business letters that received good results for me. In these times, such letters may be in the form of an email, of course. I found great results by writing professional letters to companies, politicians, and others. I have found that the keys to getting positive results and getting what you want, may include writing well, being professional, and telling the reader of your correspondence exactly what you want in the fewest amount of words possible.

Once a friend told me, "I wrote that I was unhappy with their product and they didn't even answer me." I asked, "Did you tell them what you expected them to do?" He looked confused. I followed up by telling him that he needs to tell his reader what results he expects. In my letters, I always told the reader what I expected him or her to do. Sometimes I would tell the reader of the correspondence that I expected a reimbursement for a failed product I had purchased. Sometimes I suggested that an appropriate compensation for my dissatisfaction with a purchase could be a coupon for a discounted or free item from their business. Though a company may benefit from any feedback you give them, just writing and complaining will likely not get the results you want. Suggest what the reader of the letter can do to accommodate you or to make things right for you. For me, writing has been the best way for me to communicate with a business or other place of which I interact. My advice is to let others know what your concern is and then offer solutions of which you reasonably believe they could accommodate you. You don't want the reader's private response to be: 'So what does this person want from me?'

Whether a writing is for business, pleasure, profit, or personal reasons such as keeping documentation of things going on in your life, you have an opportunity to share your thoughts through your writings. Read and write. If you aren't a good writer and need to improve your clarity of content, spelling, grammar usage, and punctuation, take time to learn it. It will be time invested well. Writing properly is essential to getting the best results possible when you are writing for another person's consumption. If you are a good writer, make it a habit of putting your writing aside for a time after you've completed the first draft, and then proofread it. Many successful writers admit that they make errors in their initial drafts. They also may admit that their errors are difficult for them to find. In particular, it can be difficult for a writer to find his or her own mistakes when the writing is fresh. I suggest putting a lengthy writing aside for many months before beginning the process of editing and rewriting it. When a writer's own writing isn't as familiar to him or her as it was when it was first written, mistakes are easier to find. As I am rewriting and expanding portions of the text in this book years after I wrote the original, I am finding a few errors and now making the necessary corrections. More than making corrections, I have rewritten passages for more clarity. For me, the longer I wait to rewrite and edit a writing, the better the final product becomes. I can only assume this is likely the case for most writers.

Another method of getting your best written product is to have someone else proofread it for you before you share it with the masses. Of course, that person should have reasonably good writing skills. Communicating via the written word can do a person a tremendous amount of good throughout life. It is time that is spent well for you and the persons who you allow to read your works.

## Chapter Thirty-Six

## Listen

To listen is a lesson that isn't easy for some people to learn well. I, for one, still need to consciously remind myself to listen to others better. Life, in general, is so much easier when one tempers his or her communications with an ample amount of listening. The best conversationalists are most often the best listeners, too.

Personally, I have a challenging time when listening to others because I don't hear well. Actually, stating that I don't hear well is indeed a gross understatement. I have a huge hearing loss in my left ear and a moderate hearing loss in my right ear. Therefore, when people are on my left side, I am often not aware that they are speaking to me unless they speak very loudly or unless I am looking in their direction and see that they are speaking to me. Even when I am aware that someone is speaking, it is much simpler for me to do the talking rather than strain to listen to someone who can't or won't speak louder.

Before one says that I need to get a hearing device, let me explain. I've tried hearing devices and they haven't worked for me in situations where I have needed hearing assistance, such as in crowded and noisy environments like a classroom, a restaurant, or in another type of crowd. Every device I've tried picks up a great amount of background noise, which doesn't help me hear who or what I am trying to or needing to hear well. As a result, I have taken the hearing aid off and just position my right ear to be as close to the speaker or sound as possible. Additionally, when I have put a hearing device on my very bad left ear, it only magnifies the muffled sound I hear naturally in that ear. The ear is damaged, and at least one ear specialist has told me that it can't be repaired. Beyond trying hearing devices, over twenty years ago, I was talked into having an inner-ear operation. Unfortunately, it was to absolutely no avail. The costly operation at Rush Hospital in Chicago didn't change a thing in relation to my ability to hear in my left ear.

Nonetheless, when my listening problem involves my inability to hear well, others could be more patient. Sadly, most people get frustrated with my poor hearing. Incredibly, some people even laugh at my situation. Sometimes I bluntly ask the rude people, "Do you laugh at people in wheelchairs, too?" My point is that an inability to hear and an inability to walk are both handicaps. Know that some people have tried most everything possible to improve their handicaps but some of them can't be corrected. Getting frustrated or laughing at a person's handicap won't change their condition. In fact, it makes their lives worse. Though a sad commentary, it is other persons who are challenged by their ability to hear that are consistently tolerant of people who are hard of hearing. Anyway, let me get off my soap box and continue with the lesson about listening.

This life's lesson is beyond the hearing problem that I and others may have. The lesson is about the times that a person does hear someone else speak. Like many, I am sometimes guilty of thinking about what I want to say next during a conversation rather than concentrating totally on what the speaker is saying to me. In order to have the best conversation possible, or a conversation that involves give and take, I have to remind myself to give the speaker my undivided attention so that I respond as appropriately as possible when it is my time to speak.

Socially, listening to others is the polite thing to do. Think about the people you like to be around. They are probably people who listen to you. They give you time to express yourself. When the conversation is turned over to them, they respond in a way that you know they listened to what you had to say. Think about the people who like to be around you, too. Likely, they are people to whom you appropriately listen when you communicate with them. You show them that you respect what they have to say by giving them equal time in a conversation. Listening has other advantages as well. By listening, one can learn a great deal, and often times it is learning more about the person or people with whom you are communicating. In conversation, balance your speaking and listening time.

# Chapter Thirty-Seven

Don't let frustrations ruin your day

Everyone experiences frustrations, whether they are from a loud neighbor who won't stifle, a terrible driver who refuses to share the road with you appropriately, an uncooperative computer's lack of a stable Wi-Fi connection, or a clerk from hell who apparently doesn't understand that you are standing in from of him or her to spend money and he or she is there to make money. Of course, frustrations come from the evils within as well, such as dissatisfaction with your waistline or rising prices at that store with the clerk from hell. Frustrations are lurking from all over and, so it appears, cannot be avoided at times. However, each person has the power to make his or her frustrations easier to cope with by tempering his or her reaction to a frustration.

Some people make a frustrating situation worse. They make the situation head further south by directing an aggressive reaction to the source of the frustration. Rather than getting into yet another confrontation with the loud neighbor, call the police and let them quiet the neighbor who thinks you want to hear rock and roll at one o'clock in the morning. Rather than driving recklessly to catch up to the terrible driver and raising your blood pressure along with your middle finger, just back off and hope that the next person the reckless driver cuts off is a police car with a police officer who will ticket him or her. Of course, if the terrible driver is so dangerously hazardous to others on the road, calling the police to report the location, driver's license, and type of car might be the best reaction. Rather than banging on the computer desk or even on the uncooperative computer, take time to restart the computer. Another solution might be to call the company responsible for the Wi-Fi connection and let them know it isn't working. The company's response may be the solution you need. As far as dealing with a clerk from hell, try not stooping to his or her level. Simply make a note of the employee's name and inform management of your concern. When I have done so, I tell management that I do not want a person to be fired for an inappropriate or bad interaction with me, but I have gone as far as to tell management that the clerk might be better suited for a job behind the scenes where the public is not subjected to him or her.

Aggressive behaviors usually don't do anything more than get a person more upset and turn the frustration into a battle that doesn't improve the situation. I try to remember to count to 10, the well-known method of calming one's self. While counting, I consider how the situation would improve if I react. Usually, the answer is that a heated reaction won't help. Honestly, if you're like me, counting to ten doesn't quite do the trick. So, maybe one might want to try count beyond 20 while taking deep breaths. Sometimes it works.

Another method of releasing personal frustrations is to write about them. Since I began writing the first edition of "Life's Lessons" some five years ago, I wrote a book entitled "My Family Won't Read My Books: About Venting Emotions." In the book with a whimsical and hopefully attention-getting title, I wrote about the extensive research I performed on the pros and cons of venting frustrations and anger. I learned a great deal about the subject and shared my newly-acquired knowledge with readers in the book. At the end of the book, I wrote about my some of my personal frustrations in life and how I try to handle them, based on the research I have done. In writing that book, I found that putting frustrations and possible solutions to the frustrations in writing can be beneficial.

Chapter Thirty-Eight

Don't brag

People can let others know their worth through their actions. People do not need to brag. While it's true that if people don't show others their positives, others may never know them. After all, other than a doting parent, it is unlikely that others are going to reveal another person's good qualities for them. In my circle of acquaintances, the mother is usually the one boasting about her children, which has become nearly expected and allowed in society with the ease of boasting on social media. Other than kids who are bragged about by their moms, however, people should let their accomplishments speak for themselves because true accomplishments often surface on their own.

When I was young, music was my main accomplishment. Yet, I never talked about it. I just kept playing my clarinet for self-enjoyment. In time, others were impressed with my ability to play. Simply do your best at what you are good at doing with the self-confidence you have earned. Rather than talk about your accomplishments, display them. If you talk about your alleged accomplishments a great deal, you appear to be conceited as well as a person with low self-esteem. A person who continually boasts and praises himself or herself to others, likely doesn't know how poor he or she comes across. However, others definitely see it.

If you can tell relatable details of your past and current accomplishments during a conversation, do it. Bide your time and there may be occasions where you can be on-topic and reveal some positive facts about yourself, your family, or a star player in your circle of acquaintances. State the facts briefly and drop it. If listeners want to know more, they will ask follow-up questions. If someone asks, you have license to elaborate. Yet, it's possible to state the facts briefly without great elaboration. By your comments being related to the ongoing conversation and only being mentioned briefly, it very likely will not come across as conceit or bragging. The key is brevity. Going on and on about your accomplishments, or the accomplishments of your children or other persons, can appear as though you're trying to overly impress others. Again, when stating your pride in yourself or someone close to you, make it factually brief when the time for such an expression of pride is appropriately relevant.

On a similar note, don't let others tell you what you should be proud of as you travel through your life's journey, as was suggested to me some twenty years ago. I remember the incident like it was yesterday because it was so impactful on me. After having taught English for about 20 years up to that point, I created my first email address in the early 1990s, and my address included the word 'teacher' in it. When I informed family, friends, and fellow-employees as to what my email address was, I was bluntly asked by someone, "Teacher? Is there nothing else that defines you?" I was shocked and momentarily didn't respond. I was incredibly offended that someone actually thought that having the word teacher within my email address wasn't appropriate in defining myself. I could have said that there are many other words or names that define me, but at that point in my life, the word teacher was among the words that defined me best. I could have also asserted that I was proud of being a teacher. Instead, I didn't respond and felt disappointed that anyone would react that way.

I suppose the lesson here is to allow your job to define you if it is a job that you feel deserves the recognition. If you have put yourself into a job as much as I have put myself into a life of educating others, it comes natural to incorporate it into other aspects of life. While it is said that there needs to be more to life than a person's work, there is nothing wrong with being proud of your profession, earnestly delving into it, and ultimately allowing that life's work partially define you. In no way did I feel it was demeaning or bragging to have incorporated the self-defining word teacher into my email address. Even though I am a retired teacher at this point in my life, I still have that email address to this day. I see no reason to change it.

Chapter Thirty-Nine

Promote yourself properly

Though it may sound somewhat contradictory after stating that one should not brag, people need to learn how to promote themselves successfully with their self-confidence, as well. Actually, it isn't contradictory at all. Proper promotion of one's self should not involve bragging. Invest time and effort in promoting yourself in a manner that gets the results you want. There are so many people who come across poorly to others, including potential employers, without apparently knowing it. They haven't figured out how to make themselves look confidently good to others.

Facebook users and other social media users see people who have never quite figured out how to promote themselves properly or positively, I'm sure. At times, the people who brag the most on social media appear to be the least self-confident, and oftentimes they come across as the people who have the very least of which to boast. People, who post practically every little thing they do, appear to have little else to do in their lives while trying desperately to convince everyone they know online that they are so extremely involved with living a life. Online, the apparently insecure people are either bragging about themselves while telling you practically every move that they, their kids, and spouse make. A logical thought for those who see these posts is to wonder when these people actually get off of their devices and spend quality time with those of whom they continuously report. Unfortunately for the chronic posters on social media, others often shake their heads and talk about such social media braggers, almost always behind their backs. Personally, I've heard that negative chatter behind others' backs and silently agree. Bragging makes no one look good.

However, I also know people with master's degrees who are doing jobs that only require a high school diploma, if even that. Incredibly, some of them take more classes and get more in debt when all they likely need to do is use some common sense in promoting themselves with the education they already have obtained. They are the opposite of a bragger. They constantly complain about their lack of decent employment and, in the process, make themselves look bad. They continually boast about the education portion of their resume while following up with an assertion that they are owed a good job with a good paycheck. Again, appropriate self-promotion of one's self should not include any sort of bragging, including bragging about one's education.

Additionally, self-promotion should not include any self-pity over the fact that a job hasn't been given yet. When one complains about the job he or she doesn't have in spite of allegedly being well-educated for so many great jobs, the person is telling people that he or she has got a problem. The person is admitting that he or she is doing something wrong. These professional students, as I call them since they spend so much time as a student in a classroom throughout their lives, error in thinking that education has to take place in the classroom. One can learn on the job, too. Illogically, some professional students insecurely state that they can't do a certain job because they never previously did that type of work. They apparently have no idea that, or refuse to accept the notion that, they can learn on the job. After all, many people apply for jobs and are given jobs that require them to learn something new. Unfortunately, this isn't apparent to some of the people who complain that they are so extremely educated but can't find a decent job.

The advice to these people is to put the college course catalog down and start making money at a job that they are qualified to have. They need to quit making excuses for bypassing jobs just because they never did that type of work before or because they think they don't know how to do it. If a person meets the educational requirements for a job, it is assumed that he or she is educable and can learn what is needed for the job of which he or she is applying. Yes, it will take work and effort to be trained for the new job.

However, it should be worth it when the person is settled into the job and finally has a decent paycheck coming in.

Once again, I have first-hand experience with this life's lesson by knowing people who fit this scenario. For years, I have suggested that one acquaintance apply for various jobs. However, he repeatedly says, "I can't do that." He says, "I never did anything like that before, and they'll want someone with experience." At that, I tirelessly repeat what I have said so many times. I tell him that I accepted many jobs through the years without having experience at the jobs. With frustration, I stress that I was trained on-the-job for practically every job I ever got, and there were so many of them including the many summer jobs throughout the teaching years. Yet, this acquaintance tells me why the job isn't a good fit and, furthermore, why he is certain he would not get the job. He adds that even if he got the job, he wouldn't like it. This professional student continues to ask what classes I would take if I were him. I keep telling him to forget about going back to school and, for now, just get a job! He is a classic example of a professional student who doesn't have a full-time professional job because he does not promote himself properly.

Another mistake I believe he has made is when he has continually told potential employers and others that he has a business background. The fact is that he has education in business, but his only business background on a job for the past several decades has been clerking at stores. When potential employers realize that his alleged-business background is no more than running a register like any high school senior is equipped to do, it has to be a negative sign to the potential employer. I have advised him to be totally honest with a potential employer and say that he has the business education but is still looking for his first professional job in business. He no longer says he has a business background in my presence, which makes me think he finally has taken some of my advice.

Another fault my acquaintance has is complaining that he is dealing with incompetent managers in his jobs. He is quick to say that he is more educated than them. While it may be true, it is totally non-productive. When he complains about the incompetence of his superiors and says they are less qualified than him to manage the store, I naturally suggest that he apply to become a manager himself. To that, he repeatedly says he doesn't want to do that. Again, the situation is a classic example of a person who does not know how to promote himself, and when given suggestions as to how he could do so better, he will not do so. He appears quite content with his constant complaining and the jobs he has, which are void of professional responsibility. There is absolutely no way I can describe him as lazy because he works a good number of hours between two low-level jobs. While he wallows in his long list of excuses for not having a professional job with a good paycheck and future, he comes across as being unmotivated and incredibly insecure. If he would promote himself properly and not shy away from taking a job in which he has to learn the responsibilities that accompany the job, his employment nightmare would end.

My advice to anyone in a situation like this is to, first, only tell everyone how much education you have once. Second, quit whining about the jobs you think you deserve but don't have. Instead, spend time looking for and applying for jobs you are educationally qualified to do. Realize that, in spite of all the time you've spent in a classroom as a student, you are most likely going to have to learn much more for the job you eventually get. Odds are that the list of obligations for the job will include skills that you've never done before, but they will be obligations you have the ability to learn and to do. Be confident in yourself. Show that confidence during the interview. Ultimately, accept the job. You need to start somewhere. You need to start sometime. Resolve to move forward in a positive direction.

Chapter Forty

Practice moderation

I finally learned that the phrase moderation in all things is more than a cliché my mother kept preaching to me through the years. It's a life's lesson worth sharing. Before I realized my obsessions myself, she saw that I would do something too much or too often without me even realizing that I was so overly engaged in something. Whether it was doing things that were good or bad for me, I would latch on to an activity and not let go of it until I would finally get sick of it or literally get sick from it. On one extreme, I would get hooked on eating a certain food. For years, my obsession with soft-serve chocolate yogurts at yogurt shops was incredible. That obsession was not moderated until the last of such shops closed near my residence and I had to travel too far to get one. On the other extreme, I would decide it was time for me to lose weight. I would diet to the point that it was most likely unhealthy for me.

When I was engaged in a songwriting project, it consumed me. Most of my free time was spent thinking about or working on a particular song. I kept a notepad and pencil by my bed for the times I would awaken during the night thinking about the latest song I was working on. As a teacher, if I was intent on getting a school project finished, it consumed me. Like the songwriting, I kept my school notepad by my bed to jot down notes when I'd wake up thinking about the project. Though I don't care to describe myself as having been obsessed, that is what I may have been with short-term projects and tasks, both personal and professional ones. Anything that I cared about was done intently. In many instances, I lacked a sense of moderation in what I was doing.

Unfortunately, I had little sense of moderation in negative aspects of life as well. When I visited the newly-opened casinos in the area, I enjoyed them and consequently went too often. It could have turned into a financial problem for me, and thank goodness, I sensed the need for moderation in entertaining gaming sooner rather than later. A bigger problem was my bad habit of smoking cigarettes. Though I was a controlled smoker at first, it became a bigger problem in time. My first effort to cut back on the nicotine was when I switched to light cigarettes from the regular ones I had been smoking. It didn't help. I found that my need for nicotine was still there, and I ended up smoking twice as many light cigarettes as I had previously been smoking the regular cigarettes. I ended up smoking two packs some days.

Beyond the incredible expense of smoking approximately a carton of cigarettes a week, I started waking up with chest pains. I reasoned that if I couldn't quit smoking, moderation would be a step in the right direction. I consciously backed off some days. Deep down, however, I knew I needed to quit smoking totally. Beyond health, friends and strangers were making comments about my constant need for a cigarette. As I sat at a coffee counter back in the day when smoking was permitted in public places, I reached for yet another cigarette. As I started lighting it, a guy sitting at the other end of the counter caught my eye and said, "Why don't you do me and yourself a favor and put that out?" I did.

There were times I would be driving down the street, get disgusted, reach under my car seat and throw the remainder of a carton of cigarettes out the window and swear I was finished. Yet, I would return to a store to buy another carton within a couple of days. I felt so defeated by not having the willpower to quit.

But then something came over me when I was about to turn 40 years old. I told myself that I was feeling too lousy for a guy who wasn't even 40 years old yet. I reasoned that if I didn't quit smoking with all of these reoccurring chest pains, I might not see many years past my 40$^{th}$ birthday. I became consumed with the desire to quit smoking by the time I would reach 40 years of age. It was the birthday present I wanted to give myself.

By the grace of God, I suppose, I was at my brother's condo in Chicago in the summer of 1989. I was in Chicago for a couple weeks with him during my summer break from school as that summer's part-time job was doing extra acting work in movies and commercials. At that particular time, I was an extra in "The Babe" starring John Goodman, which was being filmed at Wrigley Field. During the same stint, I got to do extra work for Spike Lee when he did a shoe commercial at United Center in Chicago. Never being able to sleep well away from home, I was up late at night watching my brother's television during my Chicago stay. An infomercial came on. A man was selling a little machine to help people stop smoking. Naturally, I watched it with great interest. The logic behind the machine's program made a lot of sense to me. The program was designed to allow a smoker to smoke a cigarette every time the machine made a beeping sound. The beeps would become fewer and fewer over a month-long period. By only smoking when the machine beeped, nicotine would be weaned out of my system. I was back at my own place when the machine arrived in my mailbox. The day it arrived, I turned it on. On that first day, it beeped about once every 20 minutes. Therefore, I was smoking my lungs out, as per usual. The next day, it beeped once about every 25 minutes. Naturally, by the end of the day when I turned the machine off, I had smoked fewer cigarettes without much concern. The process continued for 28 days, giving me fewer cigarettes each day as the machine slowly increased the duration of time between beeps. On the $28^{th}$ day, I turned the machine on and it played a long melody, and I figured that meant that I was down to my last cigarette. I smoked one cigarette that morning after the tune played and the machine never made another sound. Just before midnight that night, I had one more cigarette at about 11:50 because I had a feeling I would never smoke again after that day.

Though it was challenging for longer than I care to remember, I made it. I succeeded in giving myself the $40^{th}$ birthday gift of becoming the non-smoker I had wanted to become for years. It remains one of my greatest personal achievements. Incredibly, as addicted as I was to nicotine, I haven't had a cigarette since. Again, for the record, that was in early August of 1989. To this day, when I latch on to a new personal activity, I remember to moderate myself because some addictions, such as cigarettes, are terrible. I realize that I have a weakness for becoming addicted. Of course, some tasks that I have not moderated, such as my possibly compulsive desire to finish writing this updated version of "Life's Lessons" before I turn 70 years old, may have positive results.

## Chapter Forty-One

Have proper timing in your life

Know when it is time to start doing some things, to continue doing some things, and to stop doing certain things in your life. Around the age of 40, I gave thought to things I better get serious about doing because, after all, at the age of 40, I was middle-aged. I wasn't the young person I always enjoyed being anymore. It was about time I started acting my older age or to at least start thinking about acting my older age. No, 40 years old is not over the hill, but it's not like being 21 anymore.

Anyway, time was passing quickly, as it always has for me, and there were things I needed to start doing or, one day, it might be too late to do certain things. Contrarily, there were things I needed to stop doing as well. Realize that whether it is personal, professional, or social things in life, the activities should be done at their proper time for having the best opportunity of success and not having detrimental effects. As mentioned in another chapter, the one about setting goals in life, wrong timing can contribute to one's failures while proper timing can lead to one's successes.

Though a person ideally needs to wait until he or she is ready, willing, and able to do something, the only one of these three components that really matters is the 'able' part of that equation. If one is too young or too old to do something, it really doesn't matter how ready and willing a person thinks he or she is. In other words, while being ready and being willing are important, the activity is not going to get done if one is not able to do it. One's body and stamina alter throughout life. If you can't do something because your mind or body are at the wrong stage of your life, deal with that reality realistically.

On a professional level, knowing the right time to progress in work or business can be the difference between success and failure.

Depending on what you do for a living, you know when it is time to continue advancing and accelerating the career or when it is time to start stabilizing your work or business as your age may be the determining factor in deciding how you will plan to work in the future. For example, if you do physical labor, reason with yourself sooner rather than later about a different line of work that you might pursue in the years ahead. Perhaps it is time to prepare yourself to do another type of job at the same company. Start preparing for a job that will be more conducive to your approaching age, which may be accompanied by reduced physical capabilities and other aging characteristics. I knew a teacher who taught physical education, and the school's principal announced at the beginning of a school year that the teacher's position had changed. The physical education teacher would now be teaching physical education half the day and teaching students how to use computers in a classroom the other half the day. When I asked the teacher about the change, she laughed and said, "I'm getting old, Scott. I can't be in the gym all day." A few years later, her job had completely shifted from the physical education teaching job to teaching all day in a classroom. Very wisely, she saw her older years approaching, prepared herself academically for a change in her job responsibility, and was able to keep a teaching job until she reached retirement age. There's nothing wrong with aging, but not planning ahead for it can make aging difficult.

Then there are the social activities in life that one might consider altering at different times in his or her life. We have all likely witnessed at least one person of whom we have been embarrassed, as the person tries unrealistically to hold on to younger days. You won't be one of those people who embarrasses yourself, or those around you, if you have a heart-to-heart with yourself and respond appropriately to the fact that you're not in your 20s anymore. In fact, you might even be so honest with yourself that you admit that acting like you're still in your 30s or 40s is ridiculous in that those ages are so far behind you that you can scarcely see them in your mind's rearview mirror anymore. It might be wise for you to realize the time in your life when you ought to stop doing certain activities and stop acting certain ways. Replace those actions with more activities and behaviors that are more in line with how you really feel at the point you are in life. There's nothing wrong with acting your age, or responding to where you are in life, and letting others act their ages. No, you don't have to stop having fun or stop others from having a good time. You can do some fun activities that don't end up with you embarrassing yourself or even hurting yourself physically. In regard to the physical activities, if looking foolish doesn't faze you, think of it this way. You could save yourself from having to take a trip to the emergency room if you would only acknowledge your age and the limitations that possibly come with it. Simply stated, accept that there are some things in life that perhaps you shouldn't or can't do anymore. More than saving yourself from embarrassment or a trip to the emergency room, it may even save your life.

## Chapter Forty-Two

Don't waste money

Though some people say that money isn't everything and money can't buy happiness, they don't know these assertions are true unless they have some money. One of life's lessons ought to be that people should not waste their money, regardless of their financial situation. People might want to consider what they are losing when they make purchases they do not need.

It isn't logical to spend money on things that can be obtained for free. Don't spend more money than is needed to obtain what is needed or wanted. Save money for the important necessities that cost money. When it comes to the big expenses, be a bargain hunter. Often times, the free version of some things, online purchases for example, may come with slight inconveniences such as advertisements when the pay version is without ads. It is incredibly high maintenance, in my opinion, to not go for the free version with slight inconveniences. When possible, click out of the ads that come with the free versions of websites and apps in order to save some money.

If something is free somewhere, go there to obtain it. Though I'm not a hardcore coupon-cutter, when I'm confronted with one in my mailbox that I know I can use, I put it in the glove compartment of my car and use it the next time I'm shopping for the product. In recent times, if I get a coupon offer in my email's inbox that I can use, I star the email and forward it to myself to keep it visibly near the top of my emails for possible use in the future. If you personally are well-off enough that you don't need to save a little money with free versions and coupons, do it anyway. You can give that extra savings to a worthwhile cause. There must be a homeless shelter, a church, a food pantry, or something else in your area that can use the money you save.

Though I'm not nearly as frugal as I preach for others to be, I have learned some ways of spending less money. Some people go to a store and buy something before a sale ends or a coupon expires. I used to respond to time-limited sales and then realized that it was a gimmick on the part of the merchandisers. At times, I was buying things I could do without by responding to time-limited sales. Embarrassingly, when I cleared out unnecessary items from my closet a few years ago, I came across a few shirts, two jackets, and even a pair of shoes that I never put on. As I recall, most of those items were the result of a buy-one get-one free sale, also called a BOGO deal, or a sale in which the second item was half-price. Since that slap in the face of financial-waste reality, I now strongly consider my needs before responding to such offers and sales. The answer is usually that I don't really need to buy many of the things that sales tempt me to purchase. The fliers that tempt me to spend money I do not need to spend now often go in the recycle bin to avoid any temptation of wasteful spending. I have saved money and, equally beneficial, have less clutter at my residence by not purchasing items I don't really need. For the record, I took some of the extra clothes that I removed from the cluttered closet to a Goodwill store while others were dropped off at a location in Chicago where homeless people had a tent community at the time.

I have a couple acquaintances who have made snide comments about the inexpensive cars I've driven in the past when they assumed I could afford more expensive cars. I let them know that I have no need for an expensive or elaborate car. I run my cars for all they are worth. I run each one of them into the ground, as the phrase goes. It makes good sense for me to drive a car that doesn't guzzle as much gas as other vehicles do. I have never looked at my car or any of my possessions as a trophy of my success, as other people apparently consider their vehicles and possessions to be. I've been content with the Chevrolet Cavalier and the Chevrolet Cobalt, in spite of all the recalls, instead of the pricier cars on the market that some people suggest I can well-afford. Ironically, they're running around in vehicles that were much pricier when they bought them as much as

17 years ago while my car is usually replaced every five years with yet another new or lightly-used car. The frequent replacements are justified due to the amount of driving I enjoy doing on my own and involved with delivery jobs I have had.

Additionally, I've learned to not waste money on vacations that I don't necessarily want or need. Sure, it's good to get away for a change of scenery and to learn about things one might discover in other places. However, I'm not one who needs a vacation every year or even every few years. I was convinced to not take vacations all that often back in the day when I had a couple of disappointing vacations. For one, I took an expensive two-week vacation thousands of miles from home with a friend and had a lousy time. I'm almost positive I would have had a better time at home, just going on day trips for the two weeks. Even though I felt I did everything right by hiring a travel agent to schedule a well-known hotel and several entertaining events, practically everything that could go wrong did go wrong. By plane, we arrived in California in the middle of the night instead of in the evening. When we went to check into the hotel the travel agent had allegedly arranged, the desk clerk said he didn't have a room. From there, things got worse. That unpleasant vacation had me stuck away from home for two weeks via plans made by the poor travel agent who, praise the Lord, appears to no longer be in business. In fact, the entire mall where the business was located has been demolished.

With that trip and a trip to New York City that wasn't without headaches, I learned that I don't have to go far from Chicago and spend a large amount of money to experience a sense of vacationing. The New York trip, incidentally, was after my trip to California. Going to New York, I simply got in my car and took off for a week. I made no reservations, didn't use a travel agency, and things worked out much better than the vacation arranged by a travel agent. Of the unusual experiences on my New York vacation, it began with me getting off an expressway in Harlem, as I had missed my intended exit closer to Manhattan. As I was stuck in traffic on an off-ramp, a man walked out of the crowd standing on the sidewalk and started washing my windshield. Of course, knowing the Chicago area as I do, I knew the window washer would expect a tip after completing the task. I didn't have any change, so I rolled my window down and yelled, "Please stop! I don't have any change!" He ignored me and continued to wash my window both sides of my front windshield. With the traffic light still not turning green for me to drive on, he stood next to my open window and put his hand out for money. When I said, "I told you I don't have any change," he bent over my windshield, grabbed my windshield wiper and started slowly pulling it up further and further. Before he broke the windshield wiper off, I frantically took my wallet out of my pocket, opened it, grabbed a bill and thrust it toward him. I think it was a 5-dollar-bill, but it may have been a larger amount. Whatever it was, it was the first bill I got my fingers on before he broke the windshield wiper off my car. From there, the trip got better, or I would have turned the car around and headed back home in practically no time. If not home, I would have at least headed back west to a place where I would have hoped for better vacationing results.

My next memorable New York City occurrence was a couple of evenings later when I took in an off-Broadway play. It was some new Neil Simon play, I believe. Though I don't remember which one of his plays it was, I was very entertained by it. The specific event I do remember about that night was when the play ended. I escaped the press of the crowd as I left the packed theater and walked about three blocks back to my car after the play had ended. Most everyone else who left the play went in another direction. Maybe that was the direction of public transportation or a closer parking lot than I had found before the event. As it was, those who walked in my direction had parked closer to the theater than I had and were no longer with me as I neared my car. I sensed one set of footsteps following me. So I walked faster. I heard the set of footsteps behind me walking faster as well. When I got to my car and turned around, I saw a big woman who asked me in a deep voice, "Want a date?" She was obviously no lady. I politely replied, "No thanks." The person walked by me and my car and continued on. Like I said, don't waste money on things you don't need or don't want.

The next day, as Mother Nature would have it, the skies opened up and it rained hard practically all day. Therefore, I took a tour of the Manhattan area. It was raining so hard that some of the tour's highlights of the city had to be passed up. I missed the Statue of Liberty experience as well as several other travel spots that ordinarily would happen on a New York City tour. The following day, I found that I had a lot to learn about being in New York City. I sat in 57th Street traffic for what appeared to a couple of hours. As far as I could see, I was the only person driving a vehicle other than a taxi cab or a double-parked delivery truck. While downtown, I went to a restaurant and was seated with other people at a table. I had never experienced any such arrangement at a restaurant in the Chicago or anywhere else. Everyone at my table had their faces buried in newspapers. No one spoke.

After eating, I walked over to BMI for a meeting I had prearranged the day before with some counselor regarding songwriting, as I am a BMI songwriter. After the uneventful meeting, I got back out on 57th Street with all the taxi cabs again and found that my horn had gone out. Naturally, being in Manhattan without a horn left me without means of displaying frustration or communicating my intended driving maneuvers with other drivers. By day's end, I had driven to New Jersey, got a new horn installed at an auto shop, and decided not to go back to New York City. Instead, I visited a former college roommate and his family in New Jersey for a couple of days.

The most unusual part of the New Jersey stay when my friend took me to a beach, which wasn't far from his house. I loved the view of New York City and the ocean's shore from where we were walking. As we kept walking, I took in the breathtaking views. He finally said, "Paulson! Don't you ever look down?" I looked at him confused and saw an all too familiar devilish grin on his face. Then, as he had implied, I looked down at the sandy beach. Everyone there was nude but us. He got a good laugh out of having shocked me by taking me to a nude beach. He quickly explained that we had to leave because people on the beach frowned on people who came to the beach and didn't participate. I haven't been back to the Eastern states since. My friend's wife invited me, though, but I procrastinated and would now have to travel to Arizona to visit with them. I may go visit them again someday. Beyond wanting to visit with them again, I would likely enjoy seeing Arizona for the first time.

Again, a day-night trip not far from home, to some place in or near Chicago, has been quite satisfying for me. Grossly understated, I've had adventures there, too! As to travelling close to home, first and foremost, no matter how nice the hotels have been when I'm away from home, I don't sleep well away from home. Furthermore, I can't help but be price-conscious when I'm on the road. Remember? This section, which has diverted to somewhat of a travelogue, is about not wasting money. Anyway, I find it difficult to totally enjoy myself when I'm tired from sleep deprivation and somewhat conscious of over-spending. So, I have taken few long vacations but haven't denied myself long-day or occasional overnight adventures. My favorite travels or vacations away from home have lasted only a few days. I went to Nashville a couple of times and once to Las Vegas. Loving the music publishing scene in Nashville, I found those excursions to be very nice and not very pricy. One of my trips to Nashville included two songwriting acquaintances from the Chicago area which, of course, made the cost of the trip very doable since we shared expenses. The sidebar to that Nashville trip is that the two people with whom I traveled to Nashville got married years later. Again, I digress. The highlight of that trip for me was meeting at a music publisher's office and being told that I had shown him a song that was "just what B.J. Thomas was looking for, and he is in the recording studio now!" The song, "You Were With Me," unfortunately didn't make it onto B.J.'s album or anyone else's. As far as making it big as a songwriter, false hopes have been endless for me.

On my last Nashville trip, after the B.J Thomas disappointment, I travelled alone. I was asked again if I wanted a date similar to the date I was offered in New York City after going to the off-Broadway play. The inquisitive Nashville offeree wasn't nearly as scary as New York's. In case you are wondering, I politely declined the Nashville offer as well. After that exchange, I thought it may have been wiser to at least have had a conversation since she appeared to be comfortably local and may have had a knowledge of the publishing business in Nashville, which could have been beneficial to me. Furthermore, in her line of work, she may even have had some personal contacts in the business. Missed opportunity? Possibly.

Years later, my brother treated me to the Las Vegas strip, which made it quite enjoyable for me, even though I lost the contents of my wallet in the casinos without actually being robbed. I learned that what-happens-in-Vegas-stays-in-Vegas isn't necessarily true when traveling with a relative, either. My brother enjoys repeating the story about a couple trying to engage me at the Caesar's Palace bar, the location he chose for me to wait for him just before heading back to Chicago. While I was annoyed by the couple, my brother was entertained by the scene. Nonetheless, Las Vegas was a terrific trip with my brother in spite of the deposit I made at every casino we visited. Financially, the not-so-hidden message is not to vacation in Las Vegas for three entire days if you enjoy gaming.

With my car's odometer as my witness, I travel locally on a near-daily basis. I started taking these short travels even before I retired from my full-time job if I wasn't working a part-time job as well on the same day. When I was ready to retire but couldn't yet, those short trips were great diversions from my work. Living less than 30 minutes from the center of Chicago by car, taking frequent travels to interesting places has been easy to do.

When I bought my condominium, I assumed I would buy a two-bedroom instead of the one-bedroom. As it turned out, the only two-bedroom available, in the building I wanted to live in, had a view of the building's garbage dumpsters and garage. I was attracted to the building because of its proximity to Chicago and its view of the Chicago skyline from the west. At the time of purchase, I thought I would buy the one-bedroom condo and, in time, move to a two-bedroom, which would also have an east-facing view, when one would become available. In time, I forgot about moving to a two-bedroom unit because I was content with the one-bedroom. Beyond the contentment, I have enjoyed the lower property taxes and condo dues as compared to what they would have been with the unnecessary two-bedroom condo. Sidestepping unexpected and unnecessary expenses have paid off through the years. Getting what one needs rather than what one thinks he or she wants can be beneficial.

My advice is for people not to concern themselves about what others think they should be doing with their money. First, get what you need. Then, get what you want, while leaving a more-than-comfortable buffer for life's unexpected emergencies. Online, there are tools such as an emergency fund calculator, which can help one decide how much they should consider having in his or her savings account for emergencies. Currently, online research suggests that a person should at least have two-weeks' salary or $1000 in savings for emergencies, whichever is the greatest. This amount may be needed for unexpected expenses such as a car repair, a minor medical concern, or an appliance that suddenly malfunctions. Of course, for more costly unexpected concerns such as losing one's job, needing a different vehicle, having a major health issue arise, as well as other unfortunate occurrences, it is better to have even more money saved.

One should obtain what he or she needs in life while moderately obtaining and doing what one wants without overspending. One ought to keep an eye on the emergency savings and not let it fall below a threshold carefully set. The result should be an ample amount of money for necessities while moderately affording some of the luxuries desired. Most of all, by not overspending, one has a better chance of avoiding the stress and personal problems, such as difficulties in a relationship, that sometimes accompany money problems. One of my favorite entertainers of all time, Johnny Carson, once said, "The only thing that money gives you is the freedom of not worrying about money." That is a very worthwhile freedom, which is more obtainable if one doesn't waste money.

Chapter Forty-Three

Discipline yourself

Discipline comes in many forms. The primary focus of this life's lesson is financial discipline. One should discipline himself or herself to accumulate some financial savings. Another way of saying this is for a person to continually have financial goals in one's life. Besides the obvious advantage of having money when you need it most, having some savings gives incredible peace of mind. As mentioned in the chapter about not wasting money, existence without some monetary backup can be stressful on a person, detrimental to his or her health, and challenging to a person's relationships. Accumulating some financial savings is a goal worth working to achieve and maintain. As previously mentioned, some experts say that a person should have at least enough money set aside to cover two weeks of his or her expenses while others suggest savings that equals six months of their current paychecks. More conservative financial analysts suggest having even more stashed away for future needs during hardships. Put some amount of money aside, no matter how much or how little. Obviously, in the extreme, if one put away just three dollars a day, he or she has over $1000 in a year. It's a start! Beyond giving one peace of mind for mental health's sake, the whole process of disciplining one's self for a positive financial goal is worthy of one's time and effort.

Even though I might be sounding obsessed with the topic of money, I'm really not. So, enough about money – for now. Disciplining one's self is a benefit beyond watching the amount of money one spends and saves. Discipline is needed to link one's goals to one's achievements. In fact, it likely takes some degree of discipline to practice most of the life's lessons I am sharing in this book. Therefore, discipline yourself as needed to stay healthy. Discipline yourself to keep learning. Discipline yourself to get a job done. Discipline yourself to be a good person. Discipline yourself to constantly treat others the way you want to be treated by them. Discipline, discipline, discipline yourself. It isn't always easy, but it makes a person good. Beyond good, being a disciplined person makes a person honorable to one's self and others.

Chapter Forty-Four

Accept change when it can likely make improvements

Be flexible. Be willing to change for the better. Do not, however, simply change for change's sake. As a teacher for more than four decades, I have witnessed many changes in education. I have seen more changes than I care to remember yet can't forget. While a few of the changes improved education, there were many changes made that were totally ineffective or absolutely no better than the teaching methods that the changes were replacing. Unfortunately, there were times in which new programs were brought into the schools that did a worse job of teaching students. Yet, administrators stubbornly held on to the new programs, perhaps to justify the expense of initiating them. Only they can give the real reason for holding on to a new program that proved to be less effective than an old one for such a lengthy period of time. Many times throughout my teaching career, an incredible amount of time, educational financial resources, and frustration went into what appeared to be no more than a change that was only made for change's sake.

Madeline Hunter, may she rest in peace, had an alleged award-winning program that may have been very good for some teachers in some schools in some communities. Where I taught, however, it was generally rejected by teachers. Yet administrators kept the program for years. Then there was the Circle program in which a group of 15 students sat in a circle with a teacher first thing every morning. Practically every adult in the building needed to be assigned to a group because there could only be a small group for the program to allegedly be effective. Using a detailed manual of what was to be discussed, teachers would present a topic to the students. Then the teachers were to ask each student in the group: "How do you feel about that?" There were teachers who expressed great concerns about the program and said they had no business conducting such sessions because they weren't trained psychologists to deal with some of the topics as well as some of the students' comments that were coming out of the discussions. Some students had concerns about the program, too, as some didn't want to discuss their feelings openly in front of others. Yet, the Circle program continued for many years. It lasted for so many years that I lost count. Many teachers told me that they weren't doing it. One teacher told me, "If my kid had to be in a program like this at his school, I'd raise hell and have him pulled out of it." Such teachers at the school of which I was employed had their students sit in a circle so it would look like they were doing Circle if someone were to walk by their classrooms. Rather than having the Circle discussions, however, they let their students talk among themselves or work on their schoolwork. I did the program with my group of students as I was instructed to do. After all, the school had apparently just started the program the year I was hired at the school. Refusing to do anything I was told to do would not be a path to tenure in the school district, obviously. What made doing the Circle activity daily even worse was that I taught in a community where the students needed more time on educational basics. At that time, academically, many students were performing far below their expected grade level and age level. Yet, administrators demanded that the all-important first period of the school day be reserved for asking students one question on a wide variety of personal topics: "How do you feel about that?" The only students who were allowed to escape the program were in band or chorus because that was the only time of day that the music teachers could schedule their programs in our school. Many teachers felt that the students in Circle groups should have spent that time improving their reading skills, writing skills and other academic skills.

Then there was one of many new reading programs that landed in our school district. It must have cost the school district a great deal of money as it covered every grade and came with many printed materials. The reading program required that the Language Arts teachers read every word they spoke during direct instruction to their classes. The scripts to be read were in the huge teacher's manual.

One woman from the school district's administrative office visited every Language Arts class in the district to observe teachers. Her job was to ensure that every teacher was enacting this program correctly. I heard that, for contractual purposes, the woman's visit could not be called an evaluation. However, that is exactly what her visit appeared to be. She evaluated what she witnessed in classes. When I was called to the office to escort the woman to my room for my observation, or evaluation, I looked the woman squarely in the eye and said, "Let's not – and say we did." As the school secretary looked shocked that I would greet someone from the administration office in such a manner. As I was certain would happen, the administrator ignored my comment and accompanied me to my classroom for the observation. I dared to stray a little from the script when she visited my classroom. When I did, the woman looked up from her copy of the manual and twitched. At that, I got back on the script. Believe it or not, I heard about my having deviated from the script from my principal. He said, "Just read what's in the manual," but didn't make a huge deal out of it. Incredibly, we were expected to read every word that was in the manual and not alter from a word of it, or we would be criticized for not doing it that way. To this day, I don't know why they didn't just buy the program on tape and have the teachers display it on the classrooms' video screens for the students. It would have been a lot easier than having some high-salaried lady from the district's administrative office go to every Language Arts class in the district to make sure teachers were reading the manual like robots.

There was no apparent educational improvement by demanding that teachers do new programs like these with their students. In fact, the school's scores often continued to drop with the new programs. The programs which included changes in ways teachers were told to teach were usually introduced by administrators who bashed the old way of doing things. They would openly criticize teachers who dared question why a change was being made, as if it was wrong to even suggest that the old way of doing something was just as good or even better. Some authoritative figures displayed an age bias against teachers who preferred doing things the old way rather than the new, too, in spite of there being no data showing that the new way was effective at all. They tried so hard to shame teachers into accepting change for change's sake. Unfortunately, the shaming worked on the teachers who basically threw their arms up and asked with frustration, 'OK. What do I have to do?'

The questions from concerned teachers who stood their ground were always something like: Why are we changing to this? What is the benefit to the students? How will the change assist me with my teaching methods? The answers to such questions, if any were given, would usually involve the notion that today's children are not the children of the past. Without evidence, it was asserted that the students need to have more activities because, so it was believed, their attention spans were shorter than the attention spans of students in the past. The response to that was obviously that we didn't want children to be so very different than the educated and disciplined children of the past. Regardless of how times change, children still need to learn the basics and to be disciplined. Too often, the new programs gave students more freedom and more choices even though it's the trained educators who need to be making educational choices for their students. It's a big part of what they have been educated to do and what they are paid to do. While hands-on learning through engaging activities has its place in some academic disciplines more than others, obviously, it needs to be done in moderation.

At the risk of sounding old school, the truth is that students still need to sit, be still, and get educated via direct instruction that occurs in a quiet learning environment at various times throughout their school day. This needs to happen no matter how incredibly traditional that may be. Yet, as I got closer to retirement, I saw many classrooms where traditional education did not occur. The best methods of teaching have to incorporate much more than the many fun-and-games programs and activities that administrators have been convinced to buy into and are thereby forcing on their staff of educators. Out of frustration over this situation, I told one superior, who rarely saw education and discipline eye-to-eye with me, that I felt like I had to keep my classroom door shut because I was afraid I would be caught being academic with my students! After I told him that, he was somewhat more accepting of my traditional ways of teaching. Yet, it was true. In my classroom, I lived in fear of being caught not doing something interactive with the students that looked like fun-and-games to any administrator who might walk by my classroom.

Sometimes, a new and unsuccessful program would eventually be dropped to move on to yet a newer program. It was so frustrating to witness and to be a part of through the years. As time passed, it has been obvious that many traditional methods often work better than the new ways of doing things. Regardless of what type of change is being enacted, if there is no data showing that a new method is better than the old way of doing something, the change should not be made. If, by chance, the change has been made and is not making improvements within a reasonable amount of time, the change should not be kept. There is no good reason for keeping a failing change, especially when students' achievement is at stake.

Another example involving education was when many English teachers were subjected to nearly a decade of teaching reading and writing via a method called whole language. Where I taught, whole language was introduced as a program that basically had students write, write, and write some more. Incredibly, the idea was that students would learn from their own mistakes if they would just keep writing. If you know one of the many people who was a child subjected to the whole language method of learning English, don't ask them what the parts of speech are in regard to basic grammar. Don't ask them about phonics in regard to reading. They will most likely have no clue unless they decided to learn about them on their own. Furthermore, don't ask them to help a child with homework in the 2000s because a person who was subjected to the whole language method was not given the universal, basic instruction in learning how to read and write. Though there is likely still debate on the whole language approach to teaching, trust me, a learner's educational devastation caused by such a program had to have been incredibly harmful through the years.

Another case in point is when I worked for a boss who insisted that learning was to be done totally through technology. Quite incredibly, she had the staff box up all of the textbooks throughout the building. They were then thrown out. She dictated her failed belief that all education should take place on computers even though most classrooms only had two computers in them. There were carts of laptops that teachers could check out at the office, but there were many more classrooms needing materials for teaching than there were carts of laptop computers available to the teachers and their students. Additionally, consider the educational time lost by teachers needing to sign out the carts of computers from the office, unload the computers from carts in their classrooms, start the computers up, eventually shut them down, and return them to the carts for transport back to the office. It was totally illogical to discard all of the books and expect teachers throughout the building to share so few computers. After just a couple of years, educational textbooks were slowly making their way back into the school. Having thrown out the books was not only a costly error made by the powers-that-be in the school, but it also caused a very trying time for the teachers. Obviously, through it all, it was educationally costly to the students, too.

Throughout the time without textbooks, the office staff continually complained about the high number of paper copies teachers were making on the copy machine. Naturally, since there were no books allowed in classrooms and there were only a limited number of computers available, the copying of educational materials at the copier was occurring at an incredible pace. The copy machine continually broke down. One late afternoon after school, I asked the technician, who serviced the school's copier, why it continued to break down. He told me that the copy machine was not made to handle the incredible amount of copies that our school was expecting it to make on a daily basis. He guaranteed me that the school's copier would keep breaking down due to the abuse it was constantly receiving. Myself, I made regular trips to the local library in the evening to use the copier there. I just paid for the copies I made because either the line of teachers at the copy machine was too long or the machine was broken. Eventually, the boss gave every teacher a code that had to be entered into the copy machine so that she could monitor how many copies each teacher was running off. Then, the problem was that teachers were stealing the code from one another by peaking over one another's shoulder when they were at the copy machine.

During my teaching career, this was the worst situation in which someone in power forced a change on an entire staff simply to be current with technology. She apparently demanded change for change's sake without having the foresight to see how bad it would turn out. Myself, as a teacher focused on English, I fortunately had hoarded a set of the old grammar books and reading books in my classroom's locked cabinet and used them as appropriate during the failed technological years. The technology-only years subjected everyone to change for changes' sake without having the sense to see how it would negatively impact everyone. That boss also had new ways of disciplining that she forced on teachers, too. Basically, she believed the poorly-behaved students needed to be hugged and should never hear a raised voice from a teacher. As far as I know, no one ever had the nerve to tell her that there were students who turned their heads and laughed as they flashed gang signs behind her back when she hugged them. No, I'm not kidding. I swear to God it happened. I saw it myself.

Putting it mildly, her disciplinary methods didn't work. The superintendent of our school district was at a meeting at our school, and I was standing nearby when I heard the superintendent ask the school's principal, "What's going on over here? I have 16 requests so far for transfers out of your building?" The principal didn't respond. As I recall, nearly one-third of the teaching staff, about 20 teachers, ended up asking for a transfer to another school in the district after her first year as the school's leader. I didn't ask for a transfer as I thought I'd give her one more year to straighten out. I really thought she would have changed her ways after so many people indicated dissatisfaction by wanting out of there. Unfortunately, things got worse. Changing to all computers and no books, changing from the school's longtime and greatly-needed strict discipline code to hugging the worst of the poorly-behaved students, and other drastic changes were apparently changes that were made to appear contemporary. They were changes that never ever should have been made. By the end of the next school year, she was doing something else for the school district other than running any school. To complete the story, her replacement was the strictest disciplinarian I had seen in all my years of teaching, and the school immediately began to improve.

Trend-setting is obviously not the problem-solver it is purported to be by some persons. Equally, tradition isn't necessarily the bad thing some insist it is. Be leery of the supervisor who claims that times have changed. Ask the superior how he or she believes times have changed as well as how their proposed change will meet the challenges of the alleged changed times.

As a supervisor who has the power to dictate policy and make changes, know that any change being made is not only doable but also will be better for the organization. Avoid wasting the organization's finances by first researching the effectiveness that the change is expected to bring. For your own success and professional reputation in the future, as well as for the benefit of everyone who works with you, do not risk change without an absolute need for it. Beyond that, prove to yourself and others that change will make improvements by presenting reliable data to support your assertions.

Many areas of life, as in education and business in general, would be so much better if people would continue doing what has worked for years and years rather than being pressured into and shamed into reinventing the wheel over and over again. If the costly, newly-invented wheel doesn't roll any better or, like whole language, doesn't even work as well, it should be banished. The notion that tradition is bad in any aspect of life is a falsehood that should be stopped. Traditionalists who do not accept change without first questioning the benefit of the change are correct in asking. They rightfully do not want change until a new way of doing things has been tested and proven to be better.

Chapter Forty-Five

Use social media with care

Be careful when engaging with social media or doing most anything online. When I started engaging on the Internet with my postings, they were basically via websites' chat rooms and message boards in which persons could leave comments, which were most often informative or opinionated comments on a wide variety of topics. About a decade later, Facebook came along in 2004, and Twitter followed in 2006. Those platforms, as well as other social media venues, made it even more important for a person to post online with care because one's posts were more accessible to the growing number of people engaging on social media. Back then, as in current times, it was clear that one needs to be cautious when using the Internet. Being a teacher, I felt I had a responsibility to post with a high level of credibility and decency due to my position in the community. Also, when I began engaging on the Internet, word was that nothing a person ever posts is anonymous. Now, 20-some years later, the fact that online posts are not anonymous is
hopefully common knowledge to most everyone who utilizes the Internet.

In my Internet infancy, I became engaged in America Online, which was the fad in the early 1990s, with its ability for one to do email, create web pages hosted by AOL, and engage in its monitored chat rooms. There may have been message boards, as well. I don't quite remember. Those were the days, and nights. Back in the day, there was a sizable difference between the speeds of online connectivity during the daytime when many people were online and nighttime when Internet traffic was decreased. One of the first things I saw when I began my involvement with the Internet is how strangely some people misbehaved. They apparently thought and trusted that they were anonymous. Then again, perhaps they simply had no shame. The insults, lewdness, and other negative online behaviors of others often surprised me and, prior to that, I've never been one who was easily surprised by much of anything. Yet, amongst the online craziness, I cautiously linked information about myself including my interests in teaching English, my newfound interest in technology, and my passion for popular music. In fact, I hosted a website, "The Chicago Music Page," which was actually many clickable pages. The website grew in popularity for several years, as evidenced by the hundreds of thousands of visitors who visited the pages according to the counter I attached to it. Just before I cancelled my AOL account for a less costly connection that using AOL, America Online, I took the web pages down. Naturally, another reason I behaved well online, besides common decency, is because I was easily traceable with the personal information I had put online about myself. Incidentally, at the time of the writing of this book, typing the URS 'AOL.com' into a web browser still goes to the AOL website. It is not, however, the popular landline-connected Internet tool it was decades ago.

Fast forward to times when Facebook and Twitter are the rage along with other available social media outlets such as Instagram. Without having to look far, the inappropriateness of online posts and other Internet engagements is still found. Again, my advice is for people to post cautiously. Besides enjoying my pastime hobby of continually updating my website about popular music, I eventually used social media to promote my online writings on a variety of topics, primarily politics. Writing online articles became one of the ways I occupied my time after I retired from full-time teaching. My articles appeared on a website that paid me for writing. The amount of money I received every month was based on how many clicks or visits my articles received. Sometimes my political opinions got people to respond antagonistically. When people reacted negatively, I often defended my opinions and tried to engage them civilly in a discussion or debate. No longer having been a full-time teacher who needed to maintain a certain image, I was freer, or perhaps looser, with my online comments. When I needed to defend my opinions online, I did so as strongly as I felt was appropriate. I gave my reasons for my opinions with facts as there was almost always data related to the topic. This was done in hopes that my opinions would garner respect while still building my readership. Unfortunately, some people continued to blast me no matter how I defended some of my written opinions. When the site went out of business, I quit writing such articles and no longer needed to defend my political opinions. Though I lost a low-paying, work from home, part-time job when the site closed, I can only believe that my blood pressure improved without the job.

Admittedly, in the past, I engaged online with disrespectful people too long. When I am occasionally faced with a disrespectful person online now, I quickly state my dissatisfaction with his or her conduct and disengage further communication with him or her. Spotting potentially disrespectful people online is something of which I have become more proficient at doing, which means I now disengage with them sooner than I had in the past. Yet, practicing this hasn't made me perfect at disconnecting from persons of whom I have needed to disengage. Getting rid of a rude and disrespectful person online not only can control one's blood pressure somewhat, but it also can avoid wasted time spent in an argument that most likely will never be resolved. Unfortunately, stopping a conversation after having stated your case can be difficult to do after someone has pushed all your buttons, so to speak. Yet, I have learned that eventual disengagement from such a person is the best route for me to go.

Regarding the person of whom I should disengage, there are several signs that help me identify him or her. The first sign that I am in a conversation that shouldn't be taking place is when I see that the other person is totally disrespectful towards me and my opinions. They don't engage in a discussion or a debate. They only criticize me. If they begin their communication by insisting that I am stupid, or some similar adjective, this conversation is probably not going to go well. When I mention that a person is lacking respect, he or she will often claim that I am the one who is disrespectful. Even though the proof is right there on the screen, if I should choose to scroll back through the conversation, there is little chance that the offending person will admit that he or she was the first to throw a disrespectful comment. The person may even claim that the insult was a joke. That's when the person needs to be reminded that written words do not have a facial expression and that words on the screen are taken literally by a reader.

Secondly, the disrespectful person rarely allows me to explain my position or belief. All the person wants to do is tell me that I am wrong. He or she gives insults without adding substance to the exchange. The third sign, and by far the most important sign, that tells me that I am in a conversation that needs to end is when the person I am communicating with has no knowledge of the topic of which I am discussing or debating with him or her.

I find that most people who want to argue about practically everything I have to say are people who know very little, if anything, about the subject. With each passing comment, they prove that they don't have enough information to engage in the conversation they are attempting to control. Some people have argued with me endlessly about political articles I have written, and then it eventually becomes apparent that they hadn't even read my article beyond the title. Oddly, they take great delight in insisting that I am wrong or simply arguing without basis.

I wrote political articles for some five years. As mentioned elsewhere, my articles usually appeared on a website named Examiner. Approximately one-hundred of my political articles were linked to a CBS News website leading up to the presidential election of 2012. One of my most controversial articles made the top of the "Drudge Report" and was allegedly read by hundreds of thousands of people. My political articles were primarily opinionated pieces, which brought out the people who wanted to argue over my opinions. I was willing to have a civilized debate with people and can say that I even enjoyed the interactions, except for the many times I realized I was entrenched in a useless debate with a person who had basically no knowledge about the topic. Expecting my readers to have as much information on the topic as I had wasn't realistic because I researched my topics a great deal before writing. I did, however, expect people to have at least perused my article and to have gained some knowledge of the topic before insisting that I was wrong, or rudely saying that I was ignorant for what I had written. I resented those who obviously knew little to nothing about a topic yet wanted to trash the opinions of someone who had taken time and care to learn about the subject. When discontent readers blasted me, most often publicly on social media without having as much as even having finished reading my articles, I didn't reacted to them well. Now, if I happen to have a politically-engaged exchange with a person online who appears to not be well-informed, I attempt to avoid an ugly scene by disengaging with them very quickly.

It is frustrating to deal with people who are uninformed because they apparently spend more time trolling the Internet, as it is called, and causing havoc rather than updating themselves on the news of the day. To have a meaningful conversation with such people, you first have to educate them on the topic being discussed. Then, you have to prove that your knowledge is correct by itemizing the sources of your information. Next, you have to repeat your informed opinion in hopes that they will finally understand the reasoning for your opinions. Unfortunately, after educating them, listing sources, and reasserting opinions in relation to the facts on the subject, often times I find that they didn't listen to a word I said. All they want to do is continue being argumentative and even insulting. Eventually, I realize that the reason they are spending so much time trolling my posts is because few others are giving them the time of day. Now, when I'm involved with an uninformed person who just wants to talk trash instead of discuss a topic, I blatantly write, "I'm sorry. I don't have time to educate you on this topic. Perhaps we can discuss this after you have become informed." If they continue to harass, as a last resort, I use the block feature on the website.

An informed person has license to display little tolerance for a person who is uninformed or who continually states misinformation. Informed people often want to hear the opinions of other informed people. I do, as was evidenced when I encouraged engagement from my readers in the comment section of the website where my articles appeared. By engaging with informed people, one may learn more, including a clearer understanding of a person's different perspective. By discussing and debating issues of the day with informed people, I have learned a great deal. Such communications can be beneficially invigorating.

You can't change people who troll the Internet, including those whose main purpose tends to be criticizing others. What you can do is stop reading the criticisms or the misinformation from such a person and move on. I try not to let the negativity on social media devour me. I suggest that all persons filter out what annoys them online and continue searching for informative connections that give an unbiased report of the news of the day. Again, I constantly improve my time spent online by disengaging from negativity and the people who spew it. Consequently, I am becoming a happier traveler on social media.

Be careful as to what you post on social media, with whom you interact, and how you interact with others. Use social media to your advantage rather than your disadvantage. Used properly, social media can make you look good rather than confrontationally bad. Never allow your social media engagements ruin your or anyone else's day.

## Chapter Forty-Six

## Smile

I could have placed this life's lesson practically anywhere in this text. Throughout life, there have been times that I have needed to remind myself to smile. The reason I ended up putting this lesson in the mid-1990s is because this was one of the most difficult periods of my life to muster a natural smile. My mother had a stroke in the early 1990s and was greatly debilitated for a number of years. Being an extremely close-knit family, she knew this was a very difficult time not only for her but for her children as well. In the difficult times more than other times, she would remind me to smile. As a youngster, she would command, "Smile. Show those pearly whites." Back then, I thought she was telling me I was a better looking guy if I would smile. While that may have been part of the reason she wanted to see me smile more often, in adulthood I realized that her command to smile most likely had more to do with improving my mood as well as the mood of those around me.

When someone tells you to smile, I believe it is best that you do it. Most likely, they care about you. They have possibly seen you with a troubled or disturbed expression on your face and think you could be thinking about other things that could bring a more pleasant expression. Likewise, if someone you care about looks concerned or unhappy, perhaps you could do the same for him or her.

Again, by smiling, you not only might improve your mood, but it will likely improve the mood of those who are fortunate enough to see it. This is evidenced by the number of times one sees a smile returned. Spread the smiles and the good moods even if you can't think of a good reason to smile at the moment. Of course, if possible, one should give real smiles. By that, I mean, smile with more than just your mouth. Smile with your whole face including your eyes. People who are good at reading body language can detect a real smile when they see one. It has been said that 70% of a person's communication is activated through his or her body language as opposed to words. Therefore, do your best at being authentic in spreading the good cheer and give the best and most real smile you can.

Whether a smile is fake, forced, or authentic, it is universally recognized as a welcome from one person to another. Throughout the world, smiles are understood. It has been written that a smile releases chemicals in the body, such as endorphins, which makes people feel happy. A smile can reduce stress, as well. Of course, smiles can be forced. Even those smiles are better than no smile at all. A genuine smile, however, is the best, as people perceive a person with a genuine smile to be friendly, approachable, and even honest. A real smile is most often detectable by one's eyes, as the muscles around one's eyes are involved with the smile as well as the muscles that move one's mouth into a smile. Granted, there are all kinds of smiles that reveal many different human emotions, but this chapter's life lesson is about the sharing of welcoming smiles.

As an added note to this chapter, I want to mention that the first major review of "65 Life's Lessons: The Most Important Lesson from Each Year of My Life (Plus Momisms)," which was the first edition of this book, awarded me the top rating of "five stars." The reviewer, however, did express one concern, which was to write that he did not like being told to smile. With all due respect and gratitude to that reviewer, I still believe in the power of smiling and have left it in this updated version of the book, which is titled "70 Life's Lessons."

## Chapter Forty-Seven

Don't hold a grudge

Let's be logical about holding a grudge towards another person. There is a fine line between showing someone that you are upset with his or her actions for a time and turning your reaction toward the person into a grudge. To make sure we are on the same page, here, I will define grudge. A grudge is a persistent feeling of ill will or resentment that has resulted from a past insult or injury. That said, the assertion that one should never hold a grudge is difficult to insist upon because that could be construed as saying a person should never show another person that he or she is discontent with someone. There are times people have license to let someone know that they have been wronged by the person. People have the right to vehemently let another person know that one's past insulting or injurious behavior isn't going to be tolerated without a negative reaction. The length of time people can reasonably be concerned about the poor actions of others is, however, subjective.

With this life's lesson, each individual needs to trust his instinct. Consider how wronged or disappointed you were by the actions or words of another. Just as important, consider when you are ready to speak to the person civilly again. If you're not ready to continue interacting at least somewhat civilly with the person, keep your distance. If it is seen as holding a grudge, so be it. You, and only you, know when you are ready to continue interacting with the person who offended you. Depending on how badly you have been wronged, you may just need an hour to get over it. Other wrongful actions may take days, weeks, months, or even years for you to feel you are ready to deal properly with the person again. You do not want to be unnecessarily and stubbornly mad longer than you need to be because that is when it turns into the holding of a grudge. If you're over the disappointment or angriness enough, if you believe the person has gotten your intended message that you're not going to accept that treatment from him or her, and if you know you are ready to carry on in the relationship properly, there is no reason to continue the alleged grudge against the wrongdoer any longer. If you let your angriness continue longer than necessary, you may ultimately appear to be a wrongful doer, too.

Another factor to consider when staying angry is how the angriness within affects one's own health. Sometimes, holding a grudge can be more difficult on the one holding the grudge than it is on the offensive person who is the target of the anger. Personally, I get mad at people who have wronged me, and I let them know in no uncertain terms that they've angered or disappointed me. However, I don't like being mad at people at all, even when it's extremely justified. I find that being at odds with someone, of whom I really want to get along, to be difficult. Most people probably feel the same as I do in this regard. So be good to yourself and the other person by being reasonable with the length of time you display your disappointment in the person. Then force yourself to be decent to the person again, as difficult as it may be at first. Cautiously get on with your renewed relationship with the person while forgiving but not forgetting.

I can only think of one instance in which I let a grudge go on too long. I had a best friend in college who ultimately ended up being a major aggravation to me. To this day, I can't say what it was that caused the friction between us. For decades, I would cringe when someone mentioned his name or when I would come across his name in print. More than 40 years since I had seen him or talked to him, I came across his name on Facebook. I tried to remember why we ended up becoming such enemies, for lack of a better term. For the life of me, I couldn't remember. I still can't remember. Anyway, when I saw his name and photo on Facebook, I was that he has had an interesting life since we last communicated. Concentrating on the good times we shared in college, I decided to send him a friendship request. Within a day, he accepted the request. Forgiving and becoming friends again, Facebook friends anyway, feels good.

Chapter Forty-Eight

Ignore ignorance

When a superior or authoritative figure of yours tells you to do something absolutely asinine that you know will not work or will not be in anyone's best interest, quietly ignore the dictate. Do not argue and cause a fuss, but simply know it is not something of which you should properly be involved. A glaring example of this occurred when I was a teacher. There was a particular administrator with whom I rarely agreed regarding disciplinary matters involving students. My methods of disciplining were stricter than. His ways of disciplining, in my humble opinion, could best be described as ineffectively appeasing towards a student's unacceptable behaviors. This administrator gave one idiotic dictate, which few teachers under his leadership will likely ever forget. He actually instructed the teachers in his school to not break up physical fights involving students. He told the faculty to stand at a safe distance from any physical altercations among students while verbally proclaiming, "Stop! I'm a teacher!"

Seriously, teachers were told that this is how a physical altercation between two students or more should be handled. The man stressed that teachers were not to become physically involved with breaking up any fights whatsoever. Anyone who ever taught teenagers and is reading this dictate from my former principal is either still laughing hysterically or staring at this book with his or her jaw dropped. Telling two angry people to stop fighting does not work in the real world, especially when it involves two children who are each trying to prove to everyone else in the room that he or she is tougher than the other child.

Even though I was bitten by a boy when I broke up one fight and ended up on crutches when I separated two girls in the cafeteria who were about to do serious damage to one another, I can't imagine me standing there and doing nothing more than announcing, "Stop! I'm a teacher!" If that is all I had done, likely the students, their parents, and other school district authorities would have rightly criticized me for having not intervened enough. They may have even suggested that I wasn't fit for the job if I had not been more assistive in physically stopping the fights. Furthermore, if that is all I would have done, the students would probably still be fighting and I would still be standing there shouting like a fool that they need to stop because, after all, I'm a teacher. Again, don't encourage stupidity by taking part in such asinine directives. If you want results, there are times common sense overrides the directives of a boss who appears to be clueless to the matters at hand.

Another example of a superior being overridden by common sense was when I taught English as a Second Language part-time at a community college. The teachers were strictly instructed to not speak any languages except English in the classroom. The instruction was to be totally of the immersion method. The primary reason for the directive, according to the head of the department, was because any student who did not speak the foreign language would be offended. As it was, I tried to follow the rule. Yet, I quietly broke the rule when I was standing before one of many classes where all the students in the class spoke Spanish as their first language. In other words, there were no non-Spanish speakers I allegedly would be offending by occasionally speaking in Spanish. First and foremost, at the beginning of the semester when I didn't know how much English my students understood, I spoke Spanish to give routine instructions including where to go and what to do in case of an emergency, such as a fire. After all, every one of my classes were at a very low English ability level, which means they spoke practically no English. Also, if the director really wanted no Spanish spoken to these low-level classes, she could have easily assigned a teacher to the low-level groups who didn't speak any Spanish. There were several such teachers on the staff, but she assigned them to higher level classes where the students were well on their way to English fluency.

Beyond vital information for the students' safety, there were obviously times a lesson was made clearer to the class and easier for me to explain if I spoke a few words or phrases in Spanish. I could have drawn pictures on the whiteboard, done charades, or done other time-taking methods of making a point clear to the students. Of course, I could have also simply resolved that there would be some things my students would not be learning because I was not allowed to translate to Spanish to clarify an educational fact.

I learned Spanish specifically to help the Hispanic and other Latino students I had in my classes through the years. I did not plan on throwing that useful skill, which was obviously very beneficial to my students, away just because I was faced with a boss who said teachers could not speak a word of Spanish. Incredibly, she was the head of a program that had more than 95 percent Spanish-speaking students and she never went to the trouble to learn Spanish herself! Additionally, she made sure that every one of the members of her secretarial staff could speak Spanish. This was absolutely necessary so that the students could sign up for the English as a Second Language classes. Again, they were coming to the school with very little, if any, English speaking abilities. They could not possibly come to the school and deal with the woman in charge of the program because she spoke no Spanish even though you could count the non-Spanish speakers in the program's classes on the fingers of one hand with fingers left over. Yes, I broke her rule on rare occasions, and I know my students learned a great deal more from me for having done so. Furthermore, if there were ever a fire in the building, they would know how to get out of the building because I made it clear to them in Spanish!

This head of the English as a Second Language program would walk into my classes and give the students a lengthy talk a couple of times every semester. This included the talk she would give to the classes at the beginning of the semester before the students in the lowest level classes had learned any English. On one occasion, while speaking to a large group of students who had practically no idea what she was talking about, she stopped speaking to the group and turned to a student sitting up front. In her loud, deep, and demanding tone, she ordered a 20-year-old male Hispanic student to put his cell phone away. As she continued to speak to the group, he continued to hold his phone in his left hand and look down at it because he obviously had no idea as to why she yelled at him. Though I dared not tell him in Spanish what she had yelled, I was ready to walk over and put my hand over his phone so he would hopefully get the idea that he should not be looking at his phone during class. Before I could, however, the director stepped intimidatingly close to the student and repeated louder, "You need to put that phone away and not bring it out during classes. You're here to learn!" Fearfully, the student stared at her. Finally, a nearby female student who figured out or perhaps understood the directive from the director told him in Spanish to put his phone away. Believe it or not, the director then turned on the female student for having spoken Spanish by announcing, "No Spanish is to be spoken here! We are here to speak English!"

On another occasion, the director walked into my class before my class was scheduled to begin and two young female students, probably around 20 years old, were laughing and speaking Spanish to one another. The director, again in her loud and commanding monotone, lectured, "Ladies! We only speak English here!" The two looked terrified at her and then continued speaking quietly to one another in Spanish. The director shouted louder, "Ladies! We only speak English here!" As the women's eyes filled up with tears, I addressed the director and said, "This is my level one class. They don't understand English yet. That's why they're here." The director then lashed out at me, "If the state comes in and hears Spanish, our program will be shut down!" As she stormed out of the room, I couldn't help but repeat, "But they don't understand English yet!" Though I loved teaching these students who had such an incredible motivation and desire to learn in that community, I moved on to another school after dealing with that director for three years. Recently, I ran into a teacher who still teachers at that school, and she told me that the director is still there, still doesn't know how to speak a word of Spanish, and is still yelling at everyone who does. Fortunately, the school I moved to was run by a director who not only treated students and faculty with respect, but also was realistic by being flexible with the alleged rules that would allegedly get the English as a Second Language program shut down by the state. No, the program at this school was never shut down for allowing a reasonable amount of the students' first languages to be spoken.

I feel very strongly about using one's first language to assist with learning a second language when the languages have vast similarities, as English and Spanish have. Knowing stark differences between one's first and second languages can assist in avoiding errors in using a new language, as well. With these strong beliefs, and with having learned a great amount of knowledge of both languages, I wrote the book "English and Spanish: The Similarities and Differences (including a Grammar and Phonics Review)."

Again, there are times one has to ignore illogical rules, as well as the people in authority who are commanding such rules, so that a person does what is best for those involved. It is no less than ignoring stupidity because some rules are stupid when taken literally.

## Chapter Forty-Nine

Give people a second chance

We all make mistakes. Anyone who does not think he or she has made a mistake either is telling a lie, is in denial, or has a very short memory. Perhaps the person is experiencing all three. It's surprising how many people are quick to gossip with statements such as, 'Well, you know, he was fired before.' Sometimes they'll say, 'I hear he spent time in jail when he was younger.' They may claim, 'His last relationship didn't work out either.' To those assertions, I usually respond with something like, 'Well, he hasn't done anything wrong to me.' Yes, I may be curious to know where he was fired from and why, but it really doesn't matter. Yes, I may be very curious to know why he may have been in jail, but, again, it really doesn't matter because he obviously has paid his debt to society and is a free man now. As far as being in a relationship that didn't work out, it doesn't matter at all. Unless there is something majorly criminal in a person's past that very possibly has not changed within his or her being, give a person a second chance. Again, we all make mistakes. Naturally, some people have made more mistakes and bigger mistakes than other people have. Furthermore, the truth may very well be that some people have not gotten caught making their mistakes while others have. Don't label a person as being bad and don't avoid a person because of a past mistake that he or she may never make again.

Yet, beware when it comes to job opportunities. In recent years, there have been incredible stories of employers hiring people with past criminal records before hiring people who have no mistakes documented in their past. Maybe they think this is necessary. Maybe they think this is good publicity for their business. Whatever the reason, it seems wrong. If someone needs a criminal record to obtain a job, something appears to be wrong with the employer's methods of hiring employees. Intentionally giving a person with a criminal record a second chance over a person without a criminal past punishes good behavior, doesn't it? It could also somehow encourage someone to actually think there is an advantage to having a criminal record. Naturally, obtaining a criminal record is not that hard to do. What is more difficult to do is to continue through life without a criminal record. Yes, hire someone who has made mistakes in the past as there should not be discrimination against persons who have cleared up their past criminal record. However, an employer should not go out of his or her way to hire a former criminal instead of someone else simply because a person has a criminal record.

One blatant example of this involved a restaurant on the West Side of Chicago. According to news reports, the owner only hired persons with a criminal record. The restaurant, located in an area considered to be a very bad area in the city, undoubtedly could have greatly benefited people in the community by offering them jobs at the eatery. Yet, the owner insisted on only hiring persons who had felonious records and had spent time in jail. A business only staffed by felons was his advertised business model. Allegedly, for reasons apparently unrelated to the owner's hiring practices, the business closed after a short amount of time. Then again, maybe some people refused to go to the eatery based on the owner's awkward requirement for hiring workers. Yes, give people a second chance, but don't require people to need a second chance to advance when hiring employees.

## Chapter Fifty

Continue learning

Beyond the required and necessary educational updating of information needed to do your job at your place of employment, be curious about many things. By continuing to learn throughout life, a person's mind stays active. Learning can also make one more interesting, as excitement regarding what is being learned comes through to others. Learn wherever you can as learning does not have to happen in a classroom. One may have maxed out on getting a formal education for one's chosen field, but that shouldn't stop one from continuing to learn about other things through other methods. One might continue learning by doing a task. Personally, the task of writing and rewriting this book to completion has further retaught me to be dedicated and focused in my work. When a personal task, such as when I first set out to write a new book, isn't absolutely necessary, disciplining myself to complete the task can be challenging. Yet, when the task is completed, the satisfaction of the achievement is great.

I chose this particular year in my life to list continued-learning because this was the point in my life when I started learning the Spanish language. Having an influx of students coming from Mexico, I felt a personal need to be able to communicate with students who came to me with very limited or no English language skills, even though learning Spanish wasn't a requirement for my job. Being an English teacher, I found it fascinating to learn the new language and to make comparisons of the similarities and differences in the two languages. I found that sharing the similarities and differences with my students helped them learn English more easily and efficiently. Such comparisons of the two languages were a good method for me to learn Spanish as well. Unfortunately, some schools insist that only English be spoken in such classes, known as immersion, which eliminates teaching via comparisons of the two languages. Yet, I used my knowledge of the two languages to teach English when possible because I have found it to be an extremely effective way to learn English when Spanish is one's first language. Naturally, it works because the two languages are very similar by having the same letters and having similar sounds spoken, also known as phonics. Beyond learning Spanish to assist my Spanish-speaking students learn English better, an unexpected personal bonus to learning Spanish has been getting to know many Spanish speakers in public who have a desire to learn English. When they hear a non-Latino like me speaking Spanish, they appear to be drawn to me, and we communicate through our shared interest in learning a new language.

Since writing the first edition of this book, "65 Life's Lessons," I have written a book titled "English and Spanish: The Similarities and Differences (including an Extensive Grammar and Phonics Review)." The book has become my best seller of the nine books I have written in the past several years. Therefore, I have had another advantage to learning a new language at approximately 50 years of age, which is having had the knowledge to write and share an educational book about the two languages.

Some years before I began learning Spanish, I engaged in learning about computers and technology by taking college coursework at a local community college. Though knowledge of computers is often a requirement for one's professional existence now, it wasn't back in the early 1990s. Learning about computers and many of the available tools that can be used on a computer was an add-on to one's previous education when I began learning technology. Again, knowing computers, technology, and the accompanying functions are much more common decades later.

Since retiring from full-time teaching, I finally have had more time to engage in and satisfy my interest in current events and politics. I have found that these learned engagements have not only been a worthwhile education for me but have been an asset to socialization as current events can make great conversation with people who have similar interests. Within the past few year, I have also read many recently written and published novels in order to study the types of creative writings that are currently successful. This type of learning should help me become the successful novel writer I would like to become. The great thing about learning in my senior years is that I now have the choice as to what I want to learn. I am not distractedly guided into having to learn something for a job. I can learn about anything I want to learn. Unlike other times in life when I had to learn something that was required for a teacher to learn or required for one of my part-time jobs, I now have the option of choosing what I want to learn. Having this choice makes learning more interesting and even fun for me. Regardless of the formal or informal routes used to continue learning, do it. It is beneficial in many ways. Beyond learning being invigorating and keeping one's mind vibrant, new knowledge can lead to newfound successes in life while possibly making a person more interesting to others.

Chapter Fifty-One

Know yourself

By knowing yourself and living the way you are most content, you may overcome frustration. Observe your likes and dislikes, while organizing your life to suit yourself as much as possible. Devise a schedule that fits you best. Whether it's a daily, weekly, monthly, yearly, or life-long schedule, get in synch with what works best for you. Of course, you need to be considerate of others when organizing your life, especially if you're a family member or living with anyone else. For the most part, however, you don't need to conform to suit others as long as you don't hurt, neglect, or inconvenience other persons in the process.

Start out by looking closely at your daily schedule. Look for what makes the good part of your day good for you and what makes another part of the day not as good. There probably is a part of the day when you are most productive and most satisfied with yourself. Whenever that part of the day is, that is when you should do your work or whatever you are constructively doing with your time. Now, my biggest job is to sit down and write each day because writing is what I've chosen to do as a nearly full-time retiree. I find that I tend to get the most accomplished if I get on the keyboard mid-afternoon. When I hit the keyboard earlier in the day, as when I first get up, I am not as enthusiastic about getting to work. Another way of saying this is to admit that I'm not a morning person at all. If I wait until nighttime to do my writing, again, things tend not to go as well as when I spend time writing in the mid-afternoon. Through self-observation, I have found that my enthusiasm for doing most any kind of writing declines after approximately three hours of intense writing. With the regression of enthusiasm, I sense that the quality of writing diminishes as well. Therefore, after approximately three hours spent on my writing, I usually save my work and start doing something else for a time. I often return to my latest writing project in the mid-evening, after having taken time to refresh. Another factor with the three hour-limit is my eyes. Sometimes, more than needing a mental break from my writing, my eyes need to get off the computer screen.

Beyond my current chosen work being part of my daily schedule, I have found that I don't like to eat first thing in the morning. I really never have. After I've been up and about for several hours, my system is ready to consume food. So, in recent times, that's when I have eaten for the first time of the day. The next time I eat is when my stomach tells me I am hungry again. The days when I used to eat as soon as I got up, then again at noon, and then again at approximately five o'clock in the afternoon, are no longer part of my routine. If it weren't for my work schedule before retiring from teaching, I most likely never would have had such a stringent schedule for eating. Naturally, if one has a job that doesn't allow stopping at will to eat, one has to eat when they are able to do so. My decades in the classroom did not allow me to eat whenever I wanted to do so. The point is that conforming to an early breakfast, midday lunch, and early dinner never was when I always wanted to eat. For most of my life, however, that is when I had always eaten because I was not only raised on that eating schedule, but that is when I had time to eat with my work schedule as an adult. Now that I have the option of making personal choices with a freer schedule, there is no reason for me to eat at specific times. Once again, by getting to know myself, I learned when these best times to consume food occur.

I take a walk for exercise practically every day. When I started the walks more than a decade ago, I was walking during the late afternoon every day. If I dared to walk earlier or later than that time of day, I felt as though something was wrong with my schedule. I eventually realized, however, that there was no reason for me to feel that way. As exercising would have it, I started dreading late afternoons some days because, feel like it or not, that was when I was making myself take my walk. By admitting how much I was starting to dread my daily walk time, I totally blew up my walking schedule. I didn't need to have a certain time of day when I walked just because it appeared as though most people who exercise daily do their exercising at approximately the same time every day. I now sometimes walk just before or just after my first meal of the day. Sometimes I walk just before or just after I start writing for the day. I no longer make a strict rule regarding the time when I will walk each day. Some days, depending on the time of year and weather conditions, I tend to take a walk when it is pleasant outside in the evening. Regardless of the time of day I take the walk, it is stringently kept on the day's to-do list until it is completed. Sometime between the last time the clock struck midnight and the next time the clock strikes midnight, a walk is taken.

I first started taking daily walks as part of my school district's health initiative to get employees to keep fit. I signed up for the program back in the 1980s, or maybe it was in the 1990s. I forget exactly when it took place. Anyway, the idea was to walk 10,000 steps a day. I did it for the duration of the program and for quite some time thereafter. I was given a certificate and several gifts related to keeping healthy as a reward. I usually took those walks after school in the hallways of the school where I worked. Walking then and there worked well because the halls had cleared out and it invigorated me for the drive home and my evening's events. After all, when I taught full-time, I was always one of the last teachers to leave the building because I wouldn't leave the building until I was prepared for the next day. That was just me. When I taught part-time at community colleges after becoming semi-retired, I taught evening classes and was again one of the last people off campus because my class ended at the end of the schools' scheduled days. When I wasn't at a school, such as on the weekends, I would walk on a treadmill.

As mentioned elsewhere in this book, I started walking daily again on the day I fully retired from teaching. I have been doing so ever since that time. Much like the time of day that I was taking the walks in recent years, I became bored with the settings. Therefore, I changed the locations of my walks nearly daily. When I saw there was a pleasant evening or night in the forecast, I held off on walking until later in the day as I found that I really enjoyed the change of pace by walking outdoors after the sun had gone down. Currently, this is my favorite setting for a walk when the weather permits me to do so. Beyond enjoying the outdoors more than the inside of a building, with or without a treadmill, I have found that surprising myself with a different location for my walk makes the activity much more interesting. One day I walk to the local store, go up and down the aisles a bit, and then head back home. The next day, if the weather isn't as pleasant, I drive to a department store during a time of day when the store isn't too busy and walk endlessly up and down the aisles. Walking in huge department stores, two-to-three times around the inside of the outer walls of the store can equate to a lengthy walk. Some years ago, I thought my department store walks were unique and odd until I read that Aretha Franklin had been an avid fan of taking power walks through Walmart stores, too. On other days, I would go to a park or a neighborhood I haven't visited in a long time and walk there. Other times, I reluctantly return to the treadmill if weather doesn't permit a pleasant walking experience away from home. In other words, though I had been restrictive in my times and locations for taking my walks in the past, I no longer require myself to walk at a specific time and place. With flexibility, I have had a great amount of success continuing my walking and keeping them interesting for me.

Again, there are vacation plans in which people tend to conform. It isn't necessary that one take a vacation every summer or every winter break. If the mood strikes, then take a vacation. When I grew up, one of the constant questions at the beginning of a school year was asking where a person went on a summer vacation with his or her family. I always had an answer because it is something our family did each and every summer. Now, as an adult, I realize it isn't something that has to be done, and I have chosen to not leave home for a vacation every year. I go rogue by usually only taking one-day jaunts locally when I want to get away. It took time before I learned this about myself because annual summer vacations were such a big part of life for so many years. With the family, vacations were great. I have a different impression of traveling alone, naturally.

When I was a kid, nightly baths were a requirement for the kids in our family. By the time I was a teen, things changed and morning showers became the routine. However, not being a morning person, I still liked getting my bath or shower out of the way at night so I could sleep a little later in the morning. I learned that something as simple as when I showered could improve my day. Regardless of the activities one chooses to do, chooses not to do, or has to do, develop the schedule that accommodates contentment and productivity as it can lead to a happy and productive life.

Chapter Fifty-Two

Get a second opinion

Get a second opinion on anything that matters in your life. When visiting a doctor with the intent of receiving an antibiotic or some sort of advice to relieve a December's cold near the end of the year, I showed the doctor a mole of which I was concerned because it had gotten larger and darker in the recent past. The doctor looked at my forearm, squinted at it and said, "It looks all right. We'll keep an eye on it." At that, I was sent on my way.

As spring weather came months later in 2002, I had the worst allergies I had ever experienced. The worst of the symptoms was the laryngitis that I was experiencing. Obviously, I needed my voice to teach every school day. After having no success with many different over-the-counter medications to end my allergy problems, I made an appointment with an allergist. While in that doctor's office, I was told to turn my forearm over so the doctor could do an allergy test on my skin. When I turned my forearm upward so the test could be administered, the doctor saw my mole and asked, "How long have you had that?" I explained that my general physician had told me, just several months ago, not to worry about it. The allergist looked puzzled, shook his head, and then turned his head to say something to his assistant in a low voice. She looked at the mole and became wide-eyed. The doctor turned back to me and sternly said, "I'd definitely have it looked at by a dermatologist."

As my allergies improved with the medications the allergist gave me in the following days, I called a dermatologist. Though I had to wait several weeks for an opening, I finally met with the dermatologist. He immediately removed the mole, put several stitches where the mole had been, and told me to return in a week. He also said that he would have the test results on the mole by then, too. A week later, the dermatologist's assistant took me to a patient's room to have the stitches removed. She asked if I had spoken to the doctor yet. I said I hadn't. She left and quickly returned with a short stack of pamphlets for me. The one on top had the word 'Melanoma' written across the front cover in bold letters. Just after receiving those, the dermatologist entered the room and said that I would need to have surgery as soon as possible. A week to the day after that, I was in a hospital having a surgical procedure to remove the area of my arm where the mole had been as well as a lymph node in my armpit. A skin graft was performed by taking skin from my upper left leg and putting it on my arm where the mole and surrounding area had been.

For five-and-a-half years, I had blood tests and chest x-rays administered approximately once every three-to-six months to monitor whether or not the melanoma had settled and spread. Thank God, it hadn't. I was told to continue visiting a dermatologist and to have suspicious moles removed every six months. This has been my routine since my initial five-year watch ended. With damaged skin, as the dermatologists have called my skin, it appears as though I will be having dermatologist visits accompanied by the removal of suspicious-looking moles from my skin for the rest of my life.

Obviously, my primary physician was completely wrong in advising me not to worry about the mole I questioned in late 2001. I should have gotten a second opinion immediately. I didn't. Yet, as far as I know, that was the first time in my life when I witnessed a doctor making a huge mistake concerning my health. From this experience, I learned that even doctors make serious errors and that a second opinion should be sought when it comes to the important things in life such as health issues. For the record, I never returned to that primary physician. I found a new doctor after that possibly-fatal error.

Besides health issues, get second opinions on other major events occurring in life. Before getting major repairs on vehicles and appliances, get a second opinion. I was told I needed a new heating system at my residence that would have cost me thousands of dollars. The second heating professional who looked at it simply moved a few wires around and got my heater working with a couple of minutes. The cost for the repair was under $100, as I recall. When the heater completely breaks down, I know it will be a big expense. However, the first person who looked at it was going to have me purchase a new system twenty-some years ago. I had a similar experience with an air conditioner in my car that only worked sporadically. The first mechanic insisted I needed a new air conditioner at the cost of $700. After the air conditioner never worked again, I went to another mechanic. He showed me that a wire in my air conditioner had been cut! He soldered the wire at the cost of $25 and sent me on my way with the air conditioning working until I traded the car in years later. No, I never went back to Fuller's Auto Shop in Hinsdale, Illinois, again! In summation, before risking health concerns or spending huge amounts of money to repair most any possession, get a second opinion. Some people are wrong and some people are dishonest.

Chapter Fifty-Three

See a doctor

See a doctor when you don't feel well or when something doesn't seem to be right with you. As stated in the chapter about getting a second opinion, it is a very good idea to get a second opinion on the major health concerns you may have. Especially do this when you aren't comfortable with the response received from the first doctor you visited. It is said that a person should have annual physical checkups conducted by a physician. At least once a year, I am seeing a doctor for one thing or another, usually something to do with very bad cold symptoms or concerns associated with allergies, which negatively affect my breathing due to congestion and other sinus discomforts.

When seeing a doctor, I remind him or her that I haven't had blood tests administered since the last time I saw seen by a doctor. I am in a hospital's network of doctors. Therefore, my files are accessible to any doctor I see within the network. I prepare myself for potential blood tests by fasting at least eight hours before ever visiting a doctor, in anticipation of giving blood for tests while I am in the office. I usually remember to drink ample amounts of water before visiting a general physician, too, as it keeps one's veins easier to locate for the giving of blood. Additionally, my tests often include a urine sample of which a good amount of water consumed before the visit assists me with taking that test, too. Consequently, blood work and a urine sample are most often administered when I haven't visited a general physician in my doctor's network for some time. For years, my doctor has notified me that my levels are good, and therefore my medication levels remain the same after the tests. Even though I always hope that my continued walks for exercise and my somewhat strict diet to maintain a decent weight in my mature years will allow me to be taken off some medications, it hasn't happened. Though discouraged by the need to keep taking daily pills for blood pressure and cholesterol, I comfort myself by knowing that things could be worse and probably would be worse if I didn't walk and make a decent attempt to eat properly.

Yet, I know I need to do more by having an annual checkup with a general physician besides the visits I make to a doctor when I am not feeling well, which is most always in the winter months. Therefore, my advice to all, as well as myself, is to get into a routine of having annual physical checkups with a doctor in addition to the visits scheduled when not feeling as well as you want to feel.

The same can be said for seeing a dentist and an eye doctor. Myself, I am good about seeing the dentist at least twice a year for cleanings and checkups, which include x-rays. My current dentist only subjects me to x-rays once a year, which I like better than having them taken twice a year as some dentists strongly suggest. I visit my optometrist at least once a year. However, I visit the eye doctor more often than once annually when there is an eye-related concern, when I tend to need a doctor-prescribed eye medication, or when I need my contacts or glasses replaced for one reason or another. Of course, always remember to take your list of general physician-prescribed medications to your dentist and eye doctor, if you are on any such meds, too. They may need to know what meds you are on before treating you and prescribing additional medications for you. Another reminder is to always be sure to take your insurance cards and information, including your Medicare card, if applicable, to any and all doctor's visit. Also, take your calendar, of which I have in my phone, so you will be at the ready for scheduling future appointments while you are there. Lastly, beyond the corrective and preventative health factors resulting from a visit to any doctor, there is a great peace of mind that one may experience after any type of health exam.

Chapter Fifty-Four

Avoid things that harm you

The most glaring thing I have needed to avoid, literally, is the sun. There are enough times when one is naturally exposed to the sunlight and the harms it can cause one's skin. Therefore, being out in the sun for extended periods of time when it isn't necessary seems to be very unwise. After my bout with melanoma, it is obvious to me that I could have done much more to avoid the sun through the years. Now, sunbathing or simply spending too much time in the sun without sunscreen protection seems like such an unnatural and unnecessary thing to do. Regarding the use of sunscreen in the past, my disclaimer is honestly that sunscreen was not around when I was a child. If it was, I was never aware of it. Back then, people didn't concern themselves about getting too much sun. Yet, through the years, the sun obviously tried to kill me, and I can safely assume that getting too much sun is not good for others either. After all, I'm not all that different from others who live under the big yellow ball, which shines brightly on the average of 189 days a year in the Chicago area where I live. Beyond sunshine, let's just say that one needs to be cautious of anything that seems to be too good to be true, like basking in the sun all summer long, as some joys can be harmful to a person.

Beyond the sun, I found cigarette smoking to be a very unwise activity that I needed to quit. As detailed elsewhere in this text, I broke that health-destroying and expensive habit before it destroyed me. At times, I have felt like gaming at casinos was a challenge for me. In response, I quit going for long periods of time. It is satisfying for me to find other forms of entertainment that don't create an addictive behavior as well as not risking the loss of too much money. Yes, it's a challenge to stop something that one enjoys, but concentrating on the benefits of subsiding the activity can encourage one to stop doing the self-destructive activities.

According to several sources, the most common addictions in the 2000s are alcohol, tobacco or nicotine, illegal drugs as well as over-the-counter doctor-prescribed drugs, gambling or gaming, coffee, food, video games, Internet and social media usage, sex and pornography, shopping, and work. If a person can't cure his or her ills alone, there should be no shame in seeking help. After all, there can be much greater shame in self-destruction from an addiction than there is in people knowing that someone is working at curing his or her ills. On a positive note about addictions, there are professionally trained people and social groups to assist addicted persons with practically every common problem or common addiction that people can possibly encounter. See a professional or join a group if an aspect of life is causing concern with your health, safety, finances, relationships, peace of mind, or anything else you find of concern.

# Chapter Fifty-Five

## Own your mistakes

Beyond owning your own mistakes, allow others to own theirs, too. I was sitting around with a group of younger people, which has become easier to do as I get older, obviously, because there are simply more people who are younger than me in my life as I become older. In fact, I now find myself the oldest person in my immediate family. Anyway, while there were people close to my age involved in the conversation I referred to above, most persons participating in the conversation were from their teenage years to their thirties. Several times during the lively discussion, someone would say something that was not quite accurate. In fact, they would blatantly say things that were factually wrong. Then, others in the crowd would verbally pounce on the person who made the error. After this happened too many times for my comfort level, I finally asserted myself and aggressively attempted to take control of the conversation. I did this somewhat rudely as it was the only way to get a word in edgewise with several very talkative young people present. My point to the group was that there used to be a time when people could simply be told to learn from their mistakes. There was not so much blatant finger-pointing and shouting involved when asserting that someone is wrong. I did admit to the group that conversations, on occasion, seem to be more electrified and maybe even more interesting with their approach, which involves rudely insisting that someone is wrong.

However, a more cultured approach is to promote the idea that people can learn rather than be shamed from their mistakes. Additionally, by not verbally pouncing on people with apparent disgust for their mistakes or inaccuracies, embarrassment can be avoided for the persons in error. Arguments may be avoided, too, as the persons in error may attempt to save face and deflect embarrassment by refusing to admit their obvious mistakes.

Honorably own your own mistakes when you have been justifiably corrected. When correcting others, do it respectfully and let others own their mistakes. Correct people without casting shame or embarrassment upon them. Beyond more polite, it can be a more effective way of moving a conversation forward after a factual mistake has been voiced by anyone. Always remember, too, that there is a difference between an opinionated comment and a factual comment. Everyone has the right to his or her own opinion while no one should be spreading false information as being factual.

## Chapter Fifty-Six

Take risks when they likely can't harm you

Take a risk when it feels right to do so. After all, you only live once. The notion that that something may be too good to be true is not always the case, as I learned when I took one of my life's biggest risks by retiring from my full-time job. I'd had part-time jobs since I was 15 years old and then worked full-time since I was 22. Therefore, just thinking about not working, after having worked full-time for some 33 years, was an incredibly challenging thought. The offer was there, however, and I hesitantly moved forward with my plan to retire. To this day I can hardly believe how fortunate I was for making that decision and having gone through the retirement process when I did. It isn't that my career didn't have personal rewards for me, because it did. Yet, after doing basically the same type of work for so many decades, as much as 28 years at the same school, making a change in my life was welcomed. Always having been one to take a safe route regarding my professional life, opting for retirement at a somewhat early age was understandably frightening. No doubt, remaining at the same full-time job for 28 years confirms my desire to remain safely assured in my professional life. Yet, when offered the option to retire and to finally change my life greatly, it was something I didn't want to pass up.

Eventually, the retirement occurred. I enjoyed my life's change and never regretted having taken the chance. Never having been a morning person, the best of the change was that, for the first time during my adult life, I didn't have to get up by 6:30 am on weekdays. With that alone, retirement has been very good. It also has given me the chance to spend more time doing what I enjoy so much, including local travels and time spent reading and writing for pleasure, as opposed to endlessly reading and writing specifically for my teaching job.

In spite of the strong positives, it took me a while to adjust to the new life. A relative pointed out to me, just a few months after I retired, that I was miserable. I knew it, but I didn't realize how apparent it was to others. I found that the words of a former principal were incredibly true when he spoke to me at a social gathering years after he had retired and years before I was able to retire. He said, "Retirement isn't all it's cracked up to be." Though he didn't expound, I soon realized what he meant after I retired. Like him, apparently, I needed to be busy and have a worth like I did when I was teaching full-time. Being initially bored and somewhat self-dissatisfied after having retired, I went back to teaching part-time at a couple of community colleges for eight years. Those teaching experiences were totally different than I had known at the lower-grade level schools where I had previously taught full-time, and they were extremely rewarding in different ways. I found a tremendous difference in the attitudes for learning between young students who had to go to school and take English classes due to a state law and the older students at the community colleges who wanted to improve their English speaking, reading, and writing skills to improve their lives and job prospects. I was the happiest teacher I had ever been when I taught adults who really wanted and needed to learn what I had to offer them. I was able to teach without having to provide the motivational gimmicks that are used in contemporary lower-level education to get young people engaged in their schooling. What a breath of fresh air the community college teaching was for me. Additionally, I taught afternoon and evening courses, which means I could still enjoy the best part of retirement from my full-time teaching job. I didn't have to get up early in the morning.

After eight years in the community college community, I am now totally retired except for doing some online writing, writing informational and fictions books, and occasional delivery jobs. The deliveries are not only for the extra money. I do them for the joy of being outdoors and driving around with purpose, as well as to add some physical activity to my days. Something as independent as online writing, however, has not been without its headaches. The biggest problem is in writing for superiors who apparently know less about the written word than their more-experienced and more-educated writers know. After all the education and experience, it was difficult to see someone tell me that something that is right is wrong. Then, in their authoritative position, they require that a writing be changed. That, incidentally, is the biggest reason I have spent less time seeking and working for websites in need of online writers. Instead, I began satisfying my desire to write by engaging in independent projects, such as writing this and many other books. Again, what led me to this point in my part-time retirement status in which I am writing more than doing anything else, was taking that first risk of retiring from full-time teaching when I first had the opportunity to do so. If I would have let my doubts hold me back, I'd probably still be teaching full-time. I don't wish a fate of teaching nearly a half-century on anyone, least of all, on me.

My advice is for a person to only take risks in life that feel right. The risks one takes may be a welcome change as retiring from full-time teaching of teenagers was for me. Yet, if the risk taken is not all it is expect to be or not as satisfying as first thought, alter the risk much like I did when I followed up my full-time retirement with part-time jobs. Teaching part-time at community colleges, doing sporadic delivery jobs, and engaging in a wide variety of writing projects have done an excellent job of erasing the boredom I experienced after retiring from full-time teaching. As busy as I currently keep myself, nobody is telling me that I appear to be miserably bored.

## Chapter Fifty-Seven

Be inclusive

Have an attitude of inclusiveness as you engage with people through life. It is more or less the belief that states 'no man is an island.' Getting through life isn't all about me or you. Instead, it's about us. It's about all of us. Don't wait for the difficult times for this to be realized. By then, it may be too late for those around you as well as for yourself. Standing completely alone doesn't make good sense for you or the people around you.

At one time or another, everyone needs someone else. First and foremost, be that someone for others through life. When your time of need comes, God willing, someone will be ready, willing, and able to assist you as well. No matter how great life is for so very many people, there will undoubtedly come a time when we can all help one another.

This life's lesson could have been inserted in this writing long before this year, but the beginning of semi-retirement was a time when I thought about this philosophy of living even more. For me, a lot of contacts were lost and life became more singular after retirement from my full-time job. Naturally, the time when one retires is a time when a person no longer sees former co-workers nearly daily. If a person chooses full-time retirement, he or she could easily become a hermit. Even if the person has a partner at home, there is a sense of being without others. There is no good time for being too alone. There are most likely others who need you, and at some point in time, you will need them.

## Chapter Fifty-Eight

Get up and out every day

If you are physically able, get out of the house even when you think you really have nowhere to go. It never occurred to me that some people don't do this after they become retired, or semi-retired. I can't imagine not getting out or not doing something. In the community I live in, I have talked to a number of people who claim to not get out of their residences very frequently other than to check their mailboxes once in a while. I only see these people when they are checking their mailboxes. Quite often, their lack of being in a good mood supports their claim of not getting out of their residences often.

Getting out and seeing people living their daily lives can be invigorating. I find nothing changes a sour mood or a dull moment quicker than getting ready to go out and then going somewhere to physically join the living. Even if it is for a short walk, getting out of the house is a change of atmosphere that literally gives a breath of fresh air. Another positive to getting out, for me, is that I tend to find myself standing in front of my open refrigerator door when I am at home with nothing to do. I find myself doing this even when I'm not hungry. Of course, while standing there, I reach for something inside. Go figure.

Some days, a walk down the street and back or a walk through a store or mall can improve my mood. Short rides into a neighborhood that I haven't visited in a while or a jaunt to a new place in the area can ignite a quick and positive change in mood. When I take a ride, I often find a business, a park, or something interesting that I hadn't noticed previously. Other options to getting out to bust the blues at any hour is to take a trip to a restaurant, even if it's just for a cup of coffee or a bowl of soup. Some days, if I have already taken a walk and have written as much as I want to write for the moment, I find a trip to the local library to be a satisfying option. Most often at the library, I find that writing at a library computer is the welcome change of atmosphere that gets me writing again. If I don't have my flash drive with me to save my work, I email my writings to myself. Many people sit at the library with reading material or gather with others in the lounge to visit. Depending on the library, there may be free programs available that are not only of interest but often educational as well.

What stays in the back of my mind, too, is that there may come the day when I won't be able to get out and about like I do now. If that time unfortunately comes, I should be satisfied to know that I got out just about as often as I could when I was able to get out. I should have no regrets if a less mobile period in my life arrives. Again, get up and get out. Beyond never knowing what may await you out there in the world, getting out does a mind and body good.

Chapter Fifty-Nine

Be informed and share knowledge, thoughts, and beliefs

Know what's going on in the neighborhood, community, country, and world around you. Attaining knowledge, forming opinions about what's going on around you, and discussing your knowledge and opinions with others can make you a more vibrant and more interesting person. There's an old adage which says that one should not discuss politics at social events. Though discussing politics has a bad reputation according to some, talking politics socially does not have to be bad.

I was reminded of politics' bad rap as a conversation piece when I went to a birthday party at a friend's house. The host looked right at me as she announced to the guests, "No talking politics here!" I knew the message was meant for me as well as two other guests who almost always end up talking politics with me when we get together. I figured that the only reason the host looked directly at me when she announced her command was because the other two persons she was giving the message to were her close relatives. Wisely, she didn't have the nerve to directly intimidate them by directly insisting that they not talk about politics. The host, as I could gather, was quite liberal. My two friends who like to talk about politics and current events are quite conservative. Myself, I am an independent political-thinker, though I admit to leaning more conservative on some issues as I age. Therefore, I took the host's command to not discuss politics to mean that she didn't want to hear a lot of conservative talk throughout the afternoon. She didn't want to hear any arguing that might accompany political talk either. Unfortunately for her, if she was eavesdropping as she went about her host's chores, she heard a lot of political talk anyway.

Talking politics isn't a bad topic for people to engage in when they have time to relax and speak their minds. I have found that discussing most anything works best when the people having the discussion are of somewhat similar minds. However, if people are totally in synch, which rarely happens, it can be a very boring conversation. I find that talking politics is a great way for people to get to know one another better. It also is a way to get to know what is important to other people and to get to know what they think about the current ways of the world. Beyond these positive points, I usually find that when I have an in-depth discussion with people who are up to date on current events or most any other topic, I almost always learn something new.

Talking politics only gets ugly when one or more people are not open to others' opinions. When you get people of very differing opinions together who are not open to differing points of view, heated arguments can ensue. However, in the situation mentioned here, the three of us, who often take time to go off to a secluded corner to have a chat with our somewhat like-minds, have a healthy discussion which may include a debate. None of us feels as though we can't express our opinions. As always when discussing politics or anything else with these people, I feel comfortable in telling them that I do not see something the way each of them do. I am allowed to express my viewpoints without being chastised. We have a mutual respect for one another. Having respect for others in a discussion and receiving respect in return are preferred components for a conversation which may involve debate.

I enjoy sharing my attitudes and beliefs with people when having a healthy and respectful conversation on political or other issues. As long as I go into the conversation knowing that my purpose is not to change anyone's mind because, on most issues, I won't. Regardless of how much I might want to try, changing one's strong beliefs almost always does not occur. It's when others force their opinions on me, or more often times criticize or insult me for what I believe, that the conversation heads south and sometimes crashes to a halt. Likewise, if I find myself starting to preach or trying to change others' strong opinions, I find it necessary to change my ways. I don't change my opinions, necessarily, but I change my method of participating in the conversation.

As mentioned with the Internet exchanges in another entry, when I have ventured into a discussion with someone of a very different mind, I am surprised when the person becomes insulting and isn't even aware that he or she is the one who is guiding the conversation in a negative direction. It's incredible. When I am accused of taking a conversation downhill when I am not the guilty party is frustrating. However, it is not as frustrating as trying to have a discussion with an uninformed know-it-all who spews misinformation in an attempt to change others' minds. To anyone who keeps up with political news and current events on a near-daily basis, an uninformed person who acts like he or she knows it all is the very worst. It's surprising how many otherwise intelligent people fall into this category. Maybe they are this way because they don't have time to keep up with current events and politics but still need to artificially present themselves as being knowledgeable. Uninformed people who find themselves in the midst of a conversation or debate could learn something if they would just close their mouths and listen. Perhaps, at a future time, they can join a similar discussion as an informed participant. Unfortunately, some uninformed people display an insecure need to monopolize conversations of which they should not be an active participant.

The bottom line for discussing and debating politics and similar topics with knowledgeable people is simple, as a friend so wisely told me when we were nearing an argument. He said, "You know, no matter what either us thinks about this (topic) isn't going to change anything anyway." Of course, he was right and his message was clear. There is no good reason to get overly excited when discussing politics and many other topics that can become intense. As a result of his wise words, another one of our high-energy debates ended peacefully in spite of how much we disagreed.

The rules should be that people are somewhat knowledgeable about a topic before entering a discussion that only benefits from having informed participants. When entering a discussion or debate with knowledgeable people, respect for all participants is the key to experiencing an eventful conversation that ends in peace. It is nearly impossible for a person to gain respect and to add value to a verbal interaction when he or she isn't necessarily informed on the topic being discussed. One appears respectful, and avoids appearing ignorant, by knowing when to participate in a conversation and when to only listen. Alternatively, when a person is well informed, he or she should let his voice be heard in an effort to share knowledge.

## Chapter Sixty

## Compliment people

Positively, there are many people who deserve your compliments. Besides making those people feel good from receiving deserved recognition for what they have done or accomplished, it makes you look secure in your ability to let others know that they have done well. While I haven't received that many compliments through time, I have received some. When I have received a compliment, I feel great in knowing that someone has recognized my alleged efforts and possible accomplishments.

Though awards are nice, there is nothing like a sincere compliment or some type of comment from someone who appreciates you. Beyond any award I have ever received as a musician, a student, a teacher, or just being an alleged good guy, I remember the compliment I got one Sunday morning when I was driving through Joliet, my former hometown. I stopped for gas at a Speedway gas station along the main thoroughfare and walked in the store. It was packed. After I found my way to the end of the long line of customers, I heard a voice yell, "Hey, everybody! That's my favorite teacher of all time! Best teacher I ever had!" I looked around and suddenly realized that people were looking at me as I stood at the end of the line. Then I saw the clerk facing the crowd as he was pointing at me! Though it took a while for me to place the older face and voice with the student I had taught years ago, I made the connection and embarrassingly grinned as I waved to him. Thankfully, I remembered that his name was Mike by the time I got up to the register. I told him that I definitely remembered him, though it had been many years since I had seen him as a student in class. I also told him that I was glad to see he was doing well at a job. The compliment he gave me occurred years ago, probably some 15 years after I'd had him in an English class. The surprise compliment before a crowd of strangers is something that still makes me feel good. Compliments and extended courtesies from former students are moments I always remember with great affection. Give compliments. They make you and the receiver feel good. Compliments, like the people giving compliment, are appreciatively remembered for a long, long time.

## Chapter Sixty-One

Be happy

This life's lesson is an easier-said-than-done lesson. Yet, I hope your first reaction to this lesson is not to ask, "Happy about what?" No one can answer that question for you but you, of course. If necessary, think hard and find something that makes you happy. Everyone needs to conquer the blues from time to time. You might even go through extended periods of time when you feel down in the dumps, whether it's because of something as uncontrollable as the weather or because of something catastrophic that has happened in your life. As difficult as it may be to accomplish at times, fight being down or depressed.

When feeling down, I do something that makes me feel good or happy, even if it is only a short-term cure for feeling down. Sometimes I take a long ride or a walk to clear my head. Other times I go to a restaurant I have been wanting to visit or go to an entertainment venue. Sometimes, I just call a friend who I know can get my mind off of me and who can possibly even give me some good and needed laughter. The last thing I do is dwell on whatever has me feeling low. I personally find that getting my mind off of me and my latest problem can improve my mood. After all, if thinking about myself is presently disturbing because of something that has happened in or to my life, there are other things I could be thinking about at any given moment.

Though a cliché, the truth is that life really is too short to be spending it feeling unhappy or even miserable. While people need to sort out their problems, they do not need to dwell on them. At some point, a person should finish sorting problems out, or at least put his or her problems on hold for a while. Spending some amount of time unstressed is good.

Yet, if one finds himself of herself being unhappy more than just occasionally, it may be a larger concern. It has been written that happiness is an internal process. Therefore, accepting one's self as he or she is may be the first step in conquering a continued unhappiness and also the first step in finding happiness. If you cannot find happiness or contentment with the things that are going on in your life, remember that you, and only you, have the ultimate power to change your life. If you cannot be happy in the situation you are in, if at all possible, make changes.

People say, "I have to…" The truth, however, is likely that they don't have to do anything. Sometimes people need to take the pressure off themselves. There may be consequences for not doing some things, but the ultimate choice to not do something that is disrupting your life is your choice. If people continually do what they feel they have to do, and doing these things makes them unhappy, they have the power to not do it. Perhaps they only need to do things differently. If it is not people's activities that are ruining their happiness, it could be their surroundings. Likewise, people have the power to change their surroundings, too. People should not wait on other people, or even their government's actions as many people apparently do, to bring them happiness. True contentment is an individual emotion that is driven by and can be obtained by each person.

Don't confuse not being happy with not being satisfied at times. It can actually be good for a person not to be totally satisfied with himself or herself all the time. If one is always totally satisfied, he or she most likely will not try to make changes that lead to improvement in his or her life. Again, however, if unhappiness is an ongoing concern for a person, he or she needs to change what is disrupting his or her contentment in life. When people have done their best to change their lives to what they perceive to be a better and happier life, they should accept themselves at that place. Acceptance of one's self has been said to be the key for true happiness. While it is normal to have moments of being somewhat dissatisfied and to want more out of life, it can be unhealthy for a person to continually not accept what he or she has. If a person cannot be happy where he or she is in life, the person can begin to make changes. One should not live in or dwell on an unwanted past. Live in the present eyes affixed on the future. With few exceptions, happiness is obtainable.

Remember that your happiness is up to you. Do not let anyone else control your happiness because, as quickly as another person can give you happiness, he or she can take it away. Take control of your happiness.

Chapter Sixty-Two

Be generous

Give as generously as possible. Give to the less fortunate, including the homeless you may encounter in your travels. Additionally, don't be intimidated into not talking about how you give to the needy. Share the idea that giving is living. After years of helping the homeless without telling a soul, I started talking about it on occasion. After I told a couple of people about my efforts in helping homeless people, I furthermore suggested that I was going to go more public about what I was doing. I was quickly advised that I shouldn't be public about doing good things for others. An acquaintance who often boasts about his staunch religious beliefs told me that the Bible says that one helps others to serve God and not to promote one's self. I was shocked by this response as I was not telling anyone that I was helping the needy to promote myself. I simply had a desire to talk about my travels in Chicago. I was quite disappointed that someone actually thought that I was talking about my travels to boast about myself. Consequently, I stifled myself as I continued to help the homeless and other needy persons who crossed my paths.

Then I realized that the reason I wanted to tell others about my giving, besides wanting to make simple conversation, was to inspire others to do the same. When telling my stories, I was knowingly offering suggestions as to how others might engage in helping the less fortunate, too. Now, in spite of potential criticism and even ridicule for admitting I help the needy, I talk about it more freely. Unfortunately, there are people who actually do not give a favorable reaction to stories of helping needy persons. Some people are skeptical of why a needy person is in the unfortunate position he or she is in. They are the type of person who passes a panhandler who obviously needs assistance and does worse than not help the person. Instead, they condescendingly shout, "Get a job!" Most people who hear me out, however, give a favorable reaction to my travelled stories.

I am adventurous, many would say too much so, and have walked right up to a group of homeless people anywhere I may encounter them. I usually offer them food, a few dollars, or weather-protective items that I often have readily available in my car's trunk. At times, I have invited one of the homeless to go to McDonald's for a bag of burgers and cups of coffee for the group I have come across. I often am amazed at the stories homeless individuals tell me about their path to their current condition. I realize that many people will not approach strangers, perhaps out of fear. However, it takes little ingenuity for anyone who has such fear to decipher ways to help the needy in a safer and more protected manner. If it is in you help the less fortunate, do it as often as you are able. It will obviously be appreciated by them. Consider it a way of giving back for the good and the blessings you have in your life. Share the good you have that others do not have.

Again, don't be intimidated into not sharing those experiences as I had been. Share your experiences as they might inspire others to help the needy, too. I prefer helping the less fortunate people one-on-one so that I know my donation is getting to individuals in need. You may be told, as my tax advisor told me, "It's not tax deductible that way." In spite of that being true, I prefer sacrificing the tax deduction and knowing that my giving isn't going to an organization's administrative costs or elsewhere. This is just how I prefer to do it because I can see that my assistance is definitely being used by those I aim to assist.

Naturally, as far as how one gives, it is totally up to the donating individual. Rather than dropping change or dollars in a panhandler's cup or hand, I prefer taking the person inside the store or a fast food restaurant and purchasing the items or food he or she wants or needs. This prevents the panhandler from buying alcohol or drugs with the money. Obviously, I want to benefit one's life and not add to one's problems. The last time I offered to help an alleged homeless man who was turned away at the drive-thru window after the restaurant's lobby closed, the manager at the window said, "You can't order for him. He needs to be in a car." I said, "You're kidding. I'm going to pay for his food. Just take his order." She insisted, "No, you can't do that!" I pulled out of the drive-thru lane, told the man to get in my car, drove around the building and ordered his food and mine with him in my car. With the fast-food restaurant manager's elevated bad attitude, I was then allowed to buy food for the man and myself.

I'm telling this story so one can see just how difficult some people make it on the less fortunate among us. There seemed to be no good reason for the manager of the restaurant to have made me and the homeless man go to all that trouble just so he could have something to eat. The time before that when I offered to buy food for a homeless person who stood at the doorway of a fast food restaurant, I invited him into the eatery with me. I was surprised to find that all he wanted was a caramel frappe. Even though I won't waste three dollars or more on a fancy drink for myself, I accommodated him because, I reasoned, everybody needs a treat sometime and I was happy to be able to provide his. The last time I took a panhandler into Walgreens, where he was not having much luck asking for change at the front doorway, I was equally surprised at what he was wanting to purchase. I asked him what he needed and he said, "Deodorant and cologne." "Nothing else?" I asked. After encouraging him to get something to eat, he grabbed a small packet of chocolate chip cookies. Again, by helping the less fortunate one-on-one like this, I know my assistance is going towards something the person truly wants or needs.

Additionally, I have a message for the people who are in need. Help people who want to help you by being open with them. It's practically impossible to help someone who is so private that a person who wants to help a person can't contact him in the future to give help. Having seen and given change to a man standing in the middle of traffic along Cicero Avenue in Cicero, Illinois, on several occasions, I finally saw him near the McDonald's restaurant entrance nearby one afternoon. Having an opportunity to speak to him, he told me that he was currently homeless but added that he occasionally stayed with an acquaintance on the far North Side of Chicago when the weather was unbearable. As we continued speaking, he told me that he was a trained mechanic who couldn't find work. I explained that I do a great amount of driving around and often see help wanted signs. Seeing a phone in his shirt pocket, I pointed to it and said, "Give me your phone number, and I'll let you know when and where I see a help wanted sign. Then you can go apply for the job." He became awkwardly quiet. More than being secretive about where he was staying in the area as a homeless person, he didn't want to share his phone number. As it happened, on two occasions since I saw him last, I saw help wanted signs for a mechanic in the area but had no way of contacting him. It was obviously his lost opportunities because he was too private or perhaps distrusting. To receive help, he needed to help others who want to help him by providing contact information.

Another such experience involved an elderly woman who I had taught with previously. In addition to losing her teaching job, for a reason she never spoke about, she didn't have enough years on the job to have a decent retirement. Perhaps she didn't have any retirement accumulated. She didn't say, and I didn't feel it was my place to ask her. Anyway, every time I ran into her at the local library, she gave me her sad story about needing a place to live soon because she was going to be kicked out of her apartment. She said she would do any job she was capable of doing to make money to pay her rent. Even though she knows me from having taught at the same school I worked at for several years, she refused to give out her phone number when I said I would need it to contact her if I came across a job for her. She said, "Oh, I've had too many problems after giving out my personal information. I don't give it to anyone anymore." Likely with a shocked look on my face, I explained the obvious. I told her that I couldn't let her know of a possible job if she didn't provide her contact information. I added that I couldn't tell her if I came across a cheap apartment that she may be able to afford. It didn't matter.

When I saw her after that conversation, she continued to talk about how she would eventually end up living out of her car. I did not repeat that I would need her contact information to help her, as it was obvious. Instead, I simply listened politely while she repeated her story of hard times. The last time I saw her, probably in 2013, she asked if she could stay at my place. I told her that wasn't possible since my place is not big enough for both of us to have our private spaces. Confusingly, she felt comfortable enough to ask me if she could move in but not comfortable enough to give me her contact information so I could help in other ways. I almost saved the story about this woman for a possible book about how strange life and people are at times. Yet, I decided to put it in this book. Again, the lesson is that if you want or need something from people, you have to make yourself able to be found by the people who may be able to and want to help you. If you don't, it is nearly impossible for anyone to help you when opportunities arise.

Chapter Sixty-Three

Just do it

Quit saying, "I could…" or "I should…" Instead, start working toward doing whatever it is that you truly have a burning desire to do and truly believe you might be able to do. In other words, just do it! When I think of the times I procrastinated by telling myself and others what I was going to do but then never finished, it frustrates and even saddens me. I finally started telling myself that, if mankind's history repeats itself, the most productive part of my life is possibly 80 percent completed as I near 70 years of age. Consequently, I needed to quit just thinking about or talking about what I want to do. I needed to just do those things. Otherwise, it's going to be too late to get everything done that I so much want to do. Beyond advising myself in my mature years that procrastination is not good, I reflectively advise that all people make the most of their lives now instead of waiting for a time that may never come.

In my case, the most obvious procrastination was authoring books. A couple decades ago, I wrote a semi-biographical fiction book, a memoir of sorts, about growing up in the Midwest. I titled it "Walk – Don't Run" after the song released in 1963 by the instrumental group called the Ventures. As I have mentioned, I loved music more than anything else when I was growing up. While the title may have little to do with the story line, other than the fact that I love music and always have, the phrase 'walk – don't run' is good advice for any adolescent reader, my assumed primary target audience of the book. Anyway, after years of saying that 'I could' or 'I should' regarding the completion of the book, I finally put some action behind those words by setting a goal to write the book to completion. As it turned out, I wasn't satisfying with the book as it was first written, and I spent time rewriting the book. Rather than a semi-biographical fiction book, I rewrote it as an honest memoir. I am much more satisfied with the second version and have gone public with the memoir version by self-publishing it as an e-book and a paperback on Amazon. I followed that writing with "65 Life's Lessons: The Most Important Lesson from Each Year of My Life (Plus Momisms)," which is the initial release of this book, which I have entitled "70 Life's Lessons." Another seven books have been written between the time I completed the rewrite of "Walk - Don't Run" and the book you are now reading. In other words, I quit talking about my intent to write books, and I just did it! Furthermore, I am still doing it. Now, if I'm talking about my books, it isn't just talk that I have embraced in procrastination. Instead, it is a form of promotion because I want my writings to be read, and it takes promotion to make the world aware of my books' existence.

Back to the life's lesson of 'just doing it,' there are reasons that people procrastinate. One of the reasons people do not move forward to meet their goals is that they have fears. An excuse for not doing something is often a personal fear that a person may not even admit to have. Personal fears hold people back. I often see myself as too fearless, to the point that I sometimes take dangerous chances.

Another reason that people procrastinate is personal shyness. Unfortunately, there are times I feel as though I have cheated myself due to an occasional shyness that I wish I didn't have. While it can be very difficult for me to overcome an occasional inner shyness, it tends to be comfortably easy for me to challenge and erase an unwarranted fear.

To help explain, shyness and fear are not identical. Shyness is when a person feels uncomfortable, bashful, timidly self-conscious, or even insecure. Fear is a feeling one gets when he or she perceives danger or some sort of threat, which results in metabolic and organ functions that cause a person to change behavior. The changed behaviors may include running away, hiding from someone or something, or becoming immobile due to the fearful situation. That is why I say that I tend not to have fears, but I am shy at times. Anyway, when one casts potential accomplishments aside due to a fear, the result is lack of personal productivity. I wish I could handle some of my inner shyness in some situations as well as I tackle the fears that I cast aside. Sometimes, I have simply been too shy to do some of the things I want to do.

I would assume that we have all been held back from doing something at one time or another due to a fear or a shyness. Even though a set goal may scare people, it should excite them, too. The longer I live, the more I try to erase my times of being shy or fearful because I know that such times in my life are holding me back from doing all I want to do.

Courage and confidence are at the root of most fears, and I believe I have enough of both. With this belief, I continually work at the challenge of not letting any personal fears get in the way of my progress. Ideally, in spite of shyness occasionally holding me back, my list of things that I want to do will eventually end up on my list of things that I have done. Of course, some of the things on the list of things that I want to do will be transferred to the list of things I have tried to do. Not all goals, realistically, are completed to satisfaction. To move more activities from my 'to-do list' to my 'have-done list,' I need to defeat my fears or shyness. I advise that we all work diligently at ridding ourselves of fears and shyness, to become our personal bests.

By defeating as many fears and instances of shyness as possible, people allow themselves the opportunity to make progress in their lives. By succumbing to fears, people are stagnant. The way I see it, every time a person doesn't do something due to a fear, he or she loses some self-esteem. That is why I continually make an effort to confront potential fears in order to complete yet another one of my goals. Even if I fail to accomplish a goal, I find some satisfaction in knowing that I tried. Moreover, a failure can teach a person not to repeat the same mistake. Finally, let it be said that a personal failure may very well inspire a person to try again and again until he or she succeeds. Giving credit where credit is due, the proverb, "If at first you don't succeed, try, try again," allegedly goes back to 1840 when it appeared in Thomas H. Palmer's "Teacher's Manual."

Chapter Sixty-Four

Realize you are dispensable

I finally learned first-hand that I'm not indispensable. It was a tough lesson to learn after having taught for more than four decades. I personally learned this incredible truth when I, along with the rest of the community college faculty, received an email stating that a new rule was going to be instituted. This new rule had been a rumor for a couple years and, unfortunately, this was one rumor that eventually came to fruition. Every teacher in a number of academic departments at the community college, including the English department in which I had been teaching, was required to have more than a bachelor's degree in the subject they were teaching and had to take six new, additional classes. Even though I had over four decades of experience in teaching English, had my Illinois teaching certificate totally up to date, and a degree in Language Arts, those achievements suddenly were not enough to continue doing the job I had been doing for the past five years at this particular community college. Along with many others at the school who shared my semi-retired status, I was told to invest my own time and a great deal of money to complete the new course requirements. Some younger teachers begrudgingly did so because they weren't of retirement age yet and financially needed the job. Additionally, many of them worked full-time in a school district while working part-time at the community college, which meant that their school district would pay the hefty tuition for the classes. The retired teachers, including me, didn't have the luxury of turning the tuition bills in for reimbursement to anyone else. The bills were to be totally ours.

Therefore, many of the part-time teachers who were retired from full-time teaching left the school. While it still seems unfair to me that teachers were let go because they wouldn't, or couldn't, invest the time and money needed to take more classes during their retirement from full-time teaching, the bottom line was that each of us was dispensable in the opinion of those who thrust the new requirements on so many experienced educators. Incidentally, it is safe to say that most of the politicians who pass such regulations that affect educators never taught a day in their lives. That, however, is another story for another time.

When leaving that school, I couldn't help but think back to my interview for the job, which was just five years before this happened. I remembered how delighted the college's department chairman and the English department head were to hire me with my qualifications and decades of experience at that time. As it turned out at the end of my employment at the school, I was encouraged to apply for what I considered a lesser position, teaching English as a Second Language. The relatively new department head told me that, though I was over-qualified for that job, I would not need to take the new classes to teach it. Instead, I decided to try full-time retirement from teaching and gradually started devoting myself to more writing tasks such as online writing and writing books. Again, quite incredibly, if the political wheels in motion at a school can do it to me in the teaching profession after four decades of service, if it can happen to others in a wide variety of life-long professions as well.

Don't misunderstand. It's not that people should not get additional training in their chosen profession as time progresses. As educators, we have been required to constantly attend workshops, seminars, conferences, and more to keep up with trends in the field. However, dictating that six college courses needed to be taken at a teacher's expense to keep the job was seen as extremely excessive by many. One math teacher who I befriended at the community college where I taught was a younger teacher who also taught full-time in the Chicago Public Schools. After he had completed the required six classes, he said that he had never spent so much time on so much busy work during his entire time in being educated to teach. His vast education included a master's degree in math with a teaching certificate endorsed to teach special education. With unsolicited reports like this coming from him and other trusted and frustrated acquaintances in the profession, there was less incentive for teachers who didn't have to continue working for financial reasons to complete the new requirements.

At this point, I'm all right with my decision to have not continued going to school to keep that job, even though I miss my time in the classroom with students. What I don't miss about the job is all the time devoted to grading my students' essays and other writings. Anyway, since the loss of that job in 2013, staying motivated and focused is occasionally a personal challenge. After all, I no longer live by a schedule that is dictated by a school bell.

Again, the obvious lesson here is that no one is indispensable, not even a large group of experienced and educated, life-long educators who thought their teaching certificates solidified them in the jobs they had been doing for decades. Unfortunately, everyone needs to be prepared to face one's possible day of dismissal because, as cruel as it may seem, the most unexpected circumstances may let one know that they are indeed quite replaceable.

## Chapter Sixty-Five

Write a last will and testament

I try to think of chores such as writing a will as no more than any other clerical duty that needs to be completed in time. I have a good friend who is an attorney. We talk about many legal things including occasional traffic tickets, which could very possibly become one of my book topics in the future, and a person's last will and testament. We finally talked seriously about who will get my stuff when I die, if I continued to be defiant about not sitting down and itemizing details in a will. I decided that I do not want Illinois' state laws or any other laws to decide who gets my worldly possessions, including any money I may have, when I reach the end of my life's journey. Even if I agree with what the laws have lined up for a person in my circumstances, I don't want any surprises that I don't know about within the laws for me or my relatives. Additionally, I have found that everyone I talked to about the laws regarding this subject had a different take on it. Therefore, it is difficult to get definitive answers to some questions one may have as to who will get a person's stuff when he or she is gone.

Proving that this is easier said than done, I only started seriously thinking about and talking about writing a will as I neared the age at which I fully retired from teaching. I am sure that I am not unique by not wanting to think about passing away. Additionally, for some of us, it isn't all that pleasant thinking about who should be included in a will and who shouldn't be.

Anyway, my last will and testament was finally written. Many may think I wrote it somewhat late in life, but the bottom line is that I am here and it is written. Though I wrote this chapter approximately five years ago in the first addition of my "Life's Lessons" book, I still admit that I am planning to have it signed by witnesses as allegedly required. I just can't completely decide on an item or two.

A haunting experience, perhaps, but I realized that a will needed to be written for my peace of mind as well as for anyone in my immediate family who will be left behind. Currently, there is a hard copy of it at home as well as a saved document file on my computer. Needless to say, there is an edit feature on my computer's document program. Decisions, decisions, decisions, as the signature beyond my own awaits. Anyway, with a will, there should be no arguing among those you leave behind. The legacy of a peaceful family is a good thing.

## Chapter Sixty-Six

Have experiences

Throughout this book, the need to learn much throughout life is strongly promoted. Beyond the learning that takes place in school and other educational settings, however, there are many other places in which one benefits from receiving an education. More than just reading, writing, listening, studying, and researching, engage in other methods to learn about many things including life.

Interact with people and do as many activities as educationally possible to extend your knowledge beyond the written page and the spoken classroom-styled lectures and experiences. Advanced learning can be found beyond the formal education. Even more, experiencing what one has learned gives a person a solid purpose for what he or she has been taught. Experience education. While obtaining knowledge makes a life good, experiencing that knowledge makes life much better.

The times when the experiences occur needs proper placement. The experiences need to take place after the necessary learning has occurred. Preceding experiences with proper knowledge will give a person the best opportunity for having the very best, most productive, and safest knowledge-based experiences in life. In many respects, education is strongly advised before experiences should occur. Likewise, the most beneficial method of learning many of the life's lessons in this book is to follow the written information with real life experiences.

Once again, to bring my personal life into each lesson, I refer to music in this life's lesson about having experiences. Beyond having a tremendous desire to learn about music as a youngster, I have experienced it throughout my life. Those experiences have advanced my knowledge and enjoyment of music through the years. Beyond studying about music, I listened to music, played a clarinet and other musical instruments, joined musical bands, directed a school band, taught woodwind instrument lessons, wrote music and lyrics, worked part-time at radio stations, worked part-time as a nightclub disc jockey, wrote articles about music, and travelled to destinations known for their musical activities and histories. Furthermore, in recent years, I have written books about music while continually updating my knowledge and the contents of the books. While I learned a great deal about music from formal education and reading books, my knowledge of music through my own experiences taught me much more about it. Furthermore, the experiences have resulted in me appreciating and loving music more than I would have otherwise. Again, I strongly advise that one should have experiences!

# Chapter Sixty-Seven

Be trustworthy

Besides the word trust, or a form of the word trust, appearing in six other chapters in this book, it is now the focus of its own chapter. Previously mentioned, trust was used self-protectively to make sure that people are cautious of who they trust. On the one hand, I have written that a young person should trust his or her mother; on the other hand, I have warned that a person who ever is caught telling a lie should not be trusted. This chapter is not, however, about who you should trust. Instead, it is about you, and every other individual, being a trustworthy person for others. As with other lessons in this book, this lesson could have comfortably been placed most anywhere in the latter chapters, as being trustworthy is a universal characteristic that remains necessary as one's life progresses.

In the simplest form, being trustworthy is being a person with whom another can share secrets. The word trustworthy, itself, has two parts or syllables. The first is trust which means reliable. The second is worthy, which can mean honorable, among other similar words. To be a trustworthy person, then, is to be one who is honorably relied upon by another person. One incident, in which a person breaches another's trust, negatively affects the relationship forever. Close friendships and family relationships can be destroyed when one's words or actions break a trust between two people. When a person causes trust to be broken, the part of a relationship involving trust can never be fully regained. Once trust has been broken, one person may forgive another, but the relationship will never ever be the same.

Being trustworthy for others is one of the most important life's lessons. People need to keep their word and do what they say they will do. Conversely, people need not do what they say they will not do.

This isn't about being irritated that someone arrives at five minutes after seven o'clock when they said they would arrive at seven o'clock. This isn't about a person promising to give a ride to a grocery store but then suddenly cannot do as planned. Experiencing repeated incidents like these with a person may make him or her unreliable, but these are not the extremely important trustworthiness instances between people that are being discussed here.

This lesson is about someone confiding in you about personal concerns that arrive in his or her life and your need to keep the confidential information private. This is also about you promising or vowing to have an intimate relationship with another person. When a person is in a relationship that needs to be kept secret, it is more than likely a relationship that should not exist. Notice, I didn't say 'when a person is in a relationship that he or she wants to be kept secret.' I said 'when a person is in a relationship that needs to be kept secret.' There is a huge difference between the words want and need in this assertion. In summation, there are trusts that must be kept for a relationship to continue throughout life. Be trustworthy to the people in your life. Coveted trust is earned by keeping confidences and your word, as well as doing what you promise to do and promise not to do.

## Chapter Sixty-Eight

Realize the past is gone

One reason people of the world study history is to assist themselves in not repeating mistakes of the past. On a personal level, however, a person needs to put the past in proper perspective. When a personal past is good, realize that there may be many tomorrows when one can strive to continue experiencing good in life. Positively, a person can set his or her ambitions on accomplishing more personal good in the future. Do not become stagnant by being too comfortable with a successful past. A prime example is former President Jimmy Carter. Being president of the United States was not the end all of his accomplishments. Decades later, he is doing things to help people and to make the world a better place.

When a personal past is not good, appreciate that there may be many tomorrows when one can strive to be better than he or she was in the past. Past mistakes should not stop a person from trying to turn his or her life around for the better. As with a good personal past, a person can set his or her ambitions on doing personal good in the future.

Remember your past. Learn from your past. Share your past as you desire to share. However, do not let your past be your life's be-all and end-all. Rather than stabilizing on the glory days of the past or stagnating on an unattractive past, continue living. Look forward to a bright future and do your best to accomplish more. The past is not your present and future. Life continues, regardless of one's accomplishments and failings of the past. Live as though the best is yet to come. After all, your personal best may very well be yet to come.

## Chapter Sixty-Nine

Be grateful

Another word that has shown up several times in this book is the word grateful. By definition, grateful is having an appreciation for the benefits one receives. I am grateful for the many blessings I have in my life, and I feel it is extremely important to show gratitude for the blessings. Ideally, I try to remember to express gratitude to God often for all I have. After all, I am still alive, healthy, have the ability to get outside and walk, have a place to live, have food to eat, have money to purchase my needs, have family and friends, and so much more. Beyond thanking God for my blessings during the time designated for silent prayer at church on Sundays, I try to remember to thank God other times, as well. I usually have thoughts of gratitude at night when preparing to sleep. It contrasts the moment when I awaken in the morning. That is the time of day when I immediately think of what I need to do throughout the day or, now that I am semi-retired with fewer obligations, what I could do throughout the day. I decide when I will do the latest part-time job, take a walk, write, read, and do whatever else I am determined to accomplish before returning to sleep that night. Often, I finally think to express my spiritual gratitude when I have the satisfaction and comfort of another day completed.

Beyond communicating gratitude to God, the people responsible for the benefits I have in life should be expressed gratitude as well. Psychological research states that the expression of gratitude to others is very beneficial to the person expressing thanks. Showing gratitude increases the degree of happiness one has in his or her life. Personally, my mood is uplifted when I take time and effort to express sincere gratitude to someone who deserves the praise. Of the many benefits of showing gratitude, it is said that being grateful helps people in their relationships, improves their physical and psychological health, brings out their positive emotions from within while increasing empathy and reducing aggression, leads to good experiences, assists them with adversity, and improves their self-esteem. Grateful people, it is also written, even sleep better. If one thinks about these claims on the benefits of gratefulness, it makes good sense to be grateful.

Beyond the assertions of the psychological research, it is logical that one's family life, social life, and interactions with persons at work as well as strangers on the street can be improved when one shows gratitude. Showing others gratitude makes a person more likeable as a grateful person does not appear to be self-centered. Overall, a grateful person feels better about himself or herself while appearing friendlier than he or she would otherwise appear to others.

Putting this lesson of gratitude totally in perspective in this book, I sincerely thank you for reading my book!

Chapter Seventy

Learn to say no

One of the most important lessons during the mature years in my life is to say no. After having practically spent my entire adult life saying yes to people, I have learned to say no. I found this lesson to be such an appropriate and satisfying concluding chapter in "65 Life's Lessons," which was written approximately five years ago, that I am keeping it as the last lesson in "70 Life's Lessons," too. This lesson tells a person to say no when the appropriate time arrives in his or her life. After all, by one's senior years, he or she has earned that right. Be forewarned that after a lifetime of saying yes to people, saying no won't be easy. However, with practice, you will become more comfortable in saying no in an assertive, polite, and genuine manner.

Younger in life, say yes as often as possible without stripping yourself of your own needs. As your years progress, however, it is all right to let others step up and say yes more often than you say it. There comes a time when older people naturally need to slow down and start giving to themselves rather than giving of themselves all the time.

A younger relative that I adore lamented that he was talked into joining a church singing group. Whether it was for his moral support or because he thought I needed something to do in my semi-retirement status, he asked me to join the singing group, too. When I said I really didn't want to join, he pestered me to join. As much as I wanted to please him, I absolutely did not want to do it. There was a time when I could have been pressured into doing it, but that time has passed. I remember this incident as being the first time that, even under great pressure, I stood firm and refused to do something that I didn't want to do but logically could have done. I had finally gotten to the point in my life when I felt I didn't have to do most everything that others want me to do. Furthermore, I didn't allow myself to get into a long discussion or an argument about it.

When he continually asked me to join the singing group, I had absolutely no desire to get up in front of the church's congregation and sing with him and the other singers in the group. Therefore, as difficult as it was for me to refuse, I adamantly gave him a negative response every time he repeated the request. In time, thank God, he finally quit asking me to join.

His eventual, long awaited acceptance of my refusal to join the singing group was encouraging to me, though. He helped me realize that it is all right for me to say no. Admittedly, it was difficult, at first, to say no to him because there was a time when he had been generous with his time for me. When I moved into my residence decades ago, he painted the living room, which is something of which I will always be grateful. Of course, he hasn't offered to paint my living room walls again, twenty-some years later, in spite of my repeated suggestions for him to do so. Maybe if I were singing in the church group with him, the living room would have been painted again. I'm not sure.

I also have started getting the nerve to say no to people who weren't ever saying yes to me, people who had become too accustomed to me saying yes to them when they needed something. Though somewhat slow for it to dawn on me, I finally realized that some people were taking advantage of me by always expecting me to take on their tasks. Just as saying no to the relative about joining the singing group at church, I found that life continues quite well with most people even when I don't say yes to them all the time.

Regarding people who never return a favor, I have already told the story about a friend who fits this situation too well. One of his refusals to give me assistance in one of my times of need resulted in me analyzing our decades-long friendship. The analysis resulted, quite incredibly, in my realizing that he had not helped me even once in my times of need. That was compared to the reality that I had helped him with many time-consuming and laborious forms of assistance as well as helping him cope with repeated challenging events in his life. After that analysis of the friendship, I told him about my analysis of our friendship and finally started saying no to him, too. By not always saying yes to him anymore, I could give more yes responses for the people who had earned my time and effort. While always saying yes to everyone might seem admirable on the surface, such a person can end up being used repeatedly by some people. After paying your time-exhaustive dues of being the yes person you have been for people through the years, learn to say no when it feels right to do so. Especially, do this to those who have not shown appreciative decency by reciprocating the goodness when you have had a time of need.

This should not be confused with situations in which someone truly needs your assistance and has nowhere else to turn. Those situations are different and one should not say no in those instances. However, in lesser situations, give yourself permission to be selective with the yes responses without feeling unnecessarily guilty. I admit that I realized this quite late in life and consequently occasionally became bitter with persons who abused my goodness. When you know you've earned the right to say no, just say it. It doesn't make you a bad person. In fact, it may make you a better person.

A last point on this lesson is that when you say no to a person, it does not mean that you want to end a positive relationship with him or her. Politely refusing one's request for assistance, especially when the person has had no problem saying no to you, should not end an acquaintanceship. If it does, the relationship was most likely not a worthy one anyway. When you know when and to whom you should say no, you will have mastered the life's lesson of having a right to say no. When you have mastered the lesson, say it without explanation, guilt, or apology.

The Bonus Cut

Momisms

I love reading the advice moms have given their children as recalled by their children. Beyond likely being good advice for everyone, things that moms have said that are forever remembered by their children can be entertaining to read as well. With due respect to my mother and with a desire to give more advice, here are 70 of the most memorable one-liners my mom gave me when I was growing up. A reader may find a standard momism here and there, but most of these are unique by being my mom's advice and warnings to me. Momisms, which can be entertaining, are sometimes affectionately referred to as Mom's Wisdom. Thank God for mothers.

Make your parents proud.

Straighten up and fly right.

Moderation in all things.

Hold your head up.

Square your shoulders, lift your head, don't look blue, look glad instead (to a melody).

Show those teeth; with that smile, you need to show it more. (Another version of this was 'show those pearlies,' as in pearly white teeth.)

Go outside; it's nice out today.

When you're crabby, you're either sick or tired; in either case, go to bed.

Be careful what you're doing. (Another version of this was 'be careful where you go, what you're doing' which made me often wonder what she knew.)

It's nobody else's fault.

Do your best.

You don't have to get all As, but I don't want to see any Cs either.

You're going to do this (school activity) whether you want to or not; you're going to try everything once; you never know, you might like it.

Are you sure you're too sick to go to school? If you're that sick, you know you're going to have to stay in bed all day.

No TV until your homework is finished, and I want to see it when you're done.

It's got to be somewhere. Where did you leave it last?

Tell the truth or you'll be in more trouble.

It's much easier to tell the truth; you don't have to work at keeping your stories straight.

If anybody hits you, hit him back.

Don't be so rough; you don't know your own strength.

You're free and American; you can do whatever you want.

It's not that hard to pick it up off the floor and put it down the laundry chute!

Put clean underwear on every day; you never know when you'll end up in the hospital.

Don't leave that laying around!

And wash that hair, too.

There aren't many rules around here, but one is that you have to be at the dinner table by five o'clock when your father gets home.

Eat your vegetables.

Eat your bread crust, it'll curl your hair.

You've had enough of that.

Clean your plate before you leave the table, and then put it in the sink.

Don't order milk or pop; it costs too much when we're out.

Don't forget anything when we leave (the restaurant) because we don't tip much when we're on vacation, and I don't want to have to come back in here.

Be home before the street light goes on.

Sometimes life isn't fair.

Talk to your grandparents when we get there.

I don't want any arguments when it's time to leave.

I should never tell you when we're planning to do anything because if we have to change plans, you act like this.

Wipe that look off your face, mister!

You better NOT be saying that to your sister.

Leave your brother alone.

Don't you ever!

You're going to get yourself slapped into the middle of next week.

I know what you're up to!

I know where you've been!

I know what you're doing in there.

Get out of there!

Unlock this door, mister!

Turn that music down!

Those are the rules in this house. You can move out when you're 18 if you want.

Don't talk to your mother like that.

Who do you think you're talking to?

You need that mouth washed out with soap.

Because I said so.

Just wait until your father gets home!

Ask your father.

You weren't raised like that.

You won't know you don't like it until you tried it.

I'll give you something to be mad about!

Try to be pleasant, will you?

And where do you think we'll get the money for that?

You've got it too good around here and don't even know it.

Stop complaining; you have a roof over your head, clothes on your back, and something to eat.

Do you know how hard your father has to work to buy that for you?

No, kids, this time we're going somewhere your father and I want to go.

(When coming home from college on weekends) If all you're going to do, when you come home, is your laundry, don't bother coming home.

I don't know who would take care of this if I weren't here.

I'm not always going to be around.

I just want what's best for you.

It's time for bed.

You make your parents proud.

Conclusion

If you try to live life by all of these life's lessons and find yourself becoming frustrated in the effort, please don't be frustrated. As anyone who knows me well can attest, I have not mastered all of my life's lessons yet, as I am human. My goal is to continue mastering as many of these lessons as possible that my life has taught me. Working at the goal of mastering life's lessons gives me a reason to get up every morning and a reason to go to sleep every night.

Special thanks:

A special thanks to Ron Smith, who was quick to suggest after "65 Life's Lessons" was completed, that I write "70 Life's Lessons" in the future. As evidenced by this book, I acted on his suggestion.

About The Author

Scott Paulson is an award-winning American English teacher and a writer. By attending North Central College in Naperville, Illinois, he earned a bachelor's degree in speech communications accompanied by an Illinois teaching certificate to teach language arts in secondary schools and beyond. After teaching full-time in public schools for 33 years, he taught at community colleges for another 8 years in the Chicago area. His writings are primarily about his interests and knowledge of education, teaching, music, politics and life. "70 Life's Lessons" is his tenth book.

Paulson's other books are, in chronological order:

- "65 Life's Lessons: The Most Important Lesson from Each Year of My Life (plus Momisms)," which is the first edition of this book, "70 Life's Lessons."
- "Walk – Don't Run" is Paulson's childhood memoir centered on his life and historic events that took place in 1960 when he was 10 years old.
- "English and Spanish: The Similarities and Differences (including an Extensive Grammar and Phonics Review)" is an educational book designed to assist readers in learning English or Spanish by knowing the vast similarities and problematic differences between the two languages.
- "Instrumentals: The Number One Instrumental Recordings from 1950–Present" is researched music history about every instrumental recording that topped Billboard Magazine's popular music charts since 1950.
- "My Family Won't Read My Books: About Venting Emotions" is another researched writing; in this whimsically titled writing, the author discusses the pros and cons of venting angers and frustrations while revealing his efforts to relieve his own frustrations in life.

- "Restaurant Stories" details Paulson's most memorable adventures in dining, which are sometimes humorous and sometimes exasperating; lists of favorite and least favorite restaurants in the Chicago area are included.
- "My Life as a Song: The History of Recorded Music" is a historical fiction novel inspired by the author's love of music; the main character, which is a popular song, tells its life's story from its birth in 1892 to the present, while embracing and describing an entire researched history of recorded music over the past century and more.
- "Christmas Words and Phrases in English and Spanish: Palabras y Frases Navideñas en Inglés y Español" is the author's follow-up educational writing about the English and Spanish languages; Christmas and seasonal words and phrases are alphabetically listed and translated from English to Spanish as well as translated from Spanish to English.
- "Food Delivery Tales: True Stories about Delivering Restaurant Food (including How to Get a Delivery Job)" is a quick, informative, and enjoyable read in which the author shares his knowledge and adventures acquired from delivering restaurant food during his semi-retirement years.

Additionally, to his publishing credits, he has had many songs, both lyric and music, published and recorded. He has also had many articles published in magazines, newspapers, and online websites. In this work, "70 Life's Lessons," he has written his suggestions for living a good life and has accompanied them with many of his life's experiences that taught him the lessons.

Scott Paulson

Made in the USA
Monee, IL
17 November 2020